DATE DUE

ENGLISH AND SCOTTISH
BALLADS

An excellent Ballad of St. GEORGE for England,

and the King of *Egypt*'s Daughter, whom he delivered from Death, and how he slew a Monstrous Dragon, &c.

To the Tune of, Flying Fame, &c.

Licensed and Entered according to Order.

Of Hectors Deeds did Homer ſing,
 & of the ſack of ſtately Troy,
What grief fair Hellen did them bring,
 which was Sir Paris only joy:
And with my pen I muſt recite
St. Georges Deeds, an Engliſh Knight:
Againſt the Sarazens full rude
 fought he full long & many a Day,
Where many a Gyant he ſubdu'd,
 in honour of the Chriſtian way;
And after many adventures paſt,
To Egypt Land he came at laſt.

And as the Story plain doth tell,

No means there was that they could find,
 for to appeaſe the Dragons rage,
But by a Virgin pure and kind,
 whereby he might his fury ſwage;
Each Day he ſhould a Maiden eat,
 for to allay his hunger great.
This thing by art the Wiſemen found,
 which truly muſt obſerved be,
Wherefore throughout the City round,
 a Virgin pure of good Degree,
Was by the Kings Commiſſion ſtill,
Took up to ſerve the Dragons will.

Thus did the Dragon every Day

ENGLISH
AND SCOTTISH
BALLADS

Edited with an Introduction
and Critical Notes
by

ROBERT GRAVES

HEINEMANN

LONDON

Heinemann Educational Books Ltd
LONDON   MELBOURNE   TORONTO
CAPE TOWN   SINGAPORE
AUCKLAND   IBADAN

First Published 1957
Reprinted 1962, 1963

Published by
Heinemann Educational Books Ltd
15-16 Queen Street, Mayfair, London, W.1
Printed in Great Britain by Butler & Tanner Ltd
Frome and London

CONTENTS

v

BALLADS

INTRODUCTION

WHAT is a ballad? The word, brought to England by the Norman-French, was once spelled 'ballet' and meant a song to which people danced. Yet no songs go with the type of dancing now called 'ballet', and no dancing went with the ballads in this collection, though most of them date from the early fourteenth to the middle of the seventeenth century—the golden age of balladry. And already by the time of Shakespeare, who writes of a

> . . . lover,
> Sighing like furnace, with a woeful ballad
> Made to his mistress' eyebrow,

'ballad' could mean any sort of poem at all, with or without music; but usually a love poem. Even the *Song of Solomon*, another name for which is 'The Song of Songs', was sometimes known as 'The Ballad of Ballads'.

To increase this confusion, old English dance ballads are now more generally called 'folk songs'.

> If all the world were paper,
>   If all the seas were ink,
> If all the trees were bread and cheese,
>   What would we have to drink?
>
> If all the vessels ran,
>   If none but had a crack,
> If Spanish apes ate all the grapes,
>   What would we do for sack?

and:

> Come, lassies and lads, get leave from your dads
>   And away to the maypole hie;
> For every he has got his she
>   And the fiddler's standing by . . .

and so forth.

The world of folk songs and ballads is a savage and mysterious one; indeed, a great many of them, though disguised in Christian dress, belong originally to the ancient pagan witch cult—or 'Old Religion'—which fought a losing battle with Christianity until finally suppressed at the beginning of the eighteenth century. The witches, who were organised by 'covens', or groups of thirteen, would meet in wild places for their 'Sabbaths', for worship, dancing and merrymaking. Shakespeare, in *Macbeth* and *The Tempest*, shows only the black side of the Old Religion: the witches' use of magic to blight crops, cause miscarriages, kill cattle and people, and raise contrary winds. He did this because James I, then on the throne, lived in terror of the Scottish witches who, at the instigation of his political enemies, had made several attempts to poison him, and whose mass-trials he had attended in person. King James kept up his courage by constantly reminding himself that the sacred oil, with which he had been anointed at his coronation, protected him against them.

It is seldom realised that nearly all English popular festivals and games, though since christianised, once belonged to the Old Religion—together with the Fairies, Lob-lie-by-the-Fire, the Billie Blin (see *Young Beichan* 15), Robin Goodfellow, and the Blue Hag (see *Loving Mad Tom* 24). The witches' principal feasts were held on the quarter days: Easter, Midsummer, Martinmas and Yule; and on the cross-quarter days of Candlemas, May Day, Lammas and All Souls'. Festivities always began on the 'Eve' of these feasts, because in the Old Religion, as in the Jewish, a 'day' started at sundown of the previous evening. Among the games played on May Eve, the merriest feast of all, was one in which women chased men to the sound of pipes and drums:

> If all those young men were like hares on the mountain,
> Then all those pretty maidens would turn hounds, go a-hunting.

> If all those young men were like ducks on the waters,
> Then all those pretty maidens would change and turn otters . . .

A fragment of a similar ballad has been preserved in the evidence given by Isobel Gowdie of Auldearne, when tried for witchcraft in 1662. This can be restored as follows:

O, I shall go into a hare
With sorrow and sighing and mickle care,
And I shall go in the Devil's name
Aye, till I be fetchéd hame.
   —Hare, take heed of a bitch greyhound
   Will harry thee all these fells around,
   For here come I in Our Lady's name
   All but for to fetch thee hame.
Cunning and art he did not lack,
But aye her whistle would fetch him back.

Yet I shall go into a trout
With sorrow and sighing and mickle doubt,
And show thee many a merry game
Ere that I be fetchéd hame.
   —Trout, take heed of an otter lank
   Will harry thee close from bank to bank,
   For here come I in Our Lady's name
   All but for to fetch thee hame.
Cunning and art, etc.

Yet I shall go into a bee
With mickle horror and dread of thee,
And flit to hive in the Devil's name
Ere that I be fetchéd hame.
   —Bee, take heed of a swallow hen
   Will harry thee close, both butt and ben,
   For here come I in Our Lady's name
   All but for to fetch thee hame.
Cunning and art, etc.

Yet I shall go into a mouse
And haste me unto the miller's house,
There in his corn to have good game
Ere that I be fetchéd hame.
   —Mouse, take heed of a white tib-cat
   That never was baulked of mouse or rat,
   For I'll crack thy bones in Our Lady's name:
   Thus shalt thou be fetchéd hame.
Cunning and art, etc.

In another game the parts were reversed. A 'Devil', or male leader of the coven, dressed in black, with charcoal-smeared face and hands, pursued a female witch. The song went:

> O, she looked out of the window
>> As white as any milk,
> And he looked in at the window
>> As black as any silk.
>
> 'Hullo, hullo, hullo, hullo! you coal-black smith!
>> I have done you no wrong,
> I never would change my maiden state
>> That I have kept so long.
> I'd rather die a maid,
>> Yes, ere then,' she said,
> 'And be buried all in my grave,
>> Than marry a nasty, dusty, rusty, fusty coal-black smith!
> My maidenhead I'll save.'
>
> Then she became a hare,
>> A hare all on a plain,
> And he became a greyhound dog,
>> To fetch her home again.
>> *Hullo, hullo, etc.*
>
> Then she became a duck,
>> A duck all on the stream,
> And he became a greyhound dog
>> To fetch her home again.
>> *Hullo, hullo, etc.*

She then becomes a fish, as did the Maid of Slane (see *Clerk Colvill* 4), and he a brown otter. Finally he catches her.

At Easter there was egg-rolling; at Midsummer, dancing around bonfires; at All Souls', fortune-telling, bobbing for apples and round-dances; at Yule, kissing under the mistletoe, bringing in the boar's head, morris dancing, and games between Holly Boys and Ivy Girls. These were followed by a New Year Wren Hunting—'*Who'll hunt the Wren?*' cries *Robin the Bobbin*—when everyone went out into the woods hunting for a gold-crest wren, and brought it triumphantly home tied to a hoop.

Besides these festival songs, work-a-day ones were sung to ighten mechanical tasks: such as spinning, weaving, grinding corn, hoeing, and so on. Many of them were 'cumulative' ballads, elaborating a simple first verse:

> One man went to mow,
> > Went to mow a meadow,
> One man and his dog
> > Went to mow a meadow

the next verse being: '*Two men went to mow . . .*' and, finally:

Twelve men went to mow,
> Went to mow a meadow,
Twelve men, eleven men, ten men, nine men, eight men, seven men,
> six men, five men, four men, three men, two men, one man and
> his dog,
Went to mow a meadow.

Then there is *The Twelve Days of Christmas*:

> On the first day of Christmas my true love sent to me
> > A partridge in a pear-tree . . .

with gifts mounting up day by day until Twelfth Night.
 And:

> In a wood there grew a tree,
> > The finest tree that you ever did see.
> The tree was in the wood,
> > And the green grass grew around . . .

On the tree's branch (in the next stanza) is a bough; on the bough, a twig; on the twig, a nest; in the nest, an egg, etc.
 And *The Maid Freed From the Gallows*:

> O, hangman stay your hand,
> > O, stay it for awhile,
> For I perceive my sister a-coming
> > Over yonder stile.

> O, have you got the gold,
> > And will you set me free?

> Or have you come to see me hang
> All on the gallows tree?

The sister refuses to help, and so, in subsequent stanzas, do all other members of the family in turn, until the maiden's true love brings the gold and ransoms her; whereupon she curses each of her relatives in turn.

These occupational ballads include the sea-chanties sung by sailors while hauling at the ropes. There was always a song-leader who stood on a platform in the fore-bitts, started each new verse and conducted the chorus. For example:

> They call me Hanging Johnny—
> *Away, boys, away!*
> They say I hanged a mony[1]—
> *Then hang, boys, hang!*
>
> They say I hanged my brother—
> *Away, boys, away!*
> They say I hanged my mother—
> *Then hang, boys, hang!*
>
> They say I hanged my Annie—
> *Away, boys, away!*
> I hanged her up so canny—
> *Then hang, boys, hang!*
>
> They say I hanged my daddy—
> *Away, boys, away!*
> But I never hanged no body—
> *Then hang, boys, hang!*

Another of these chanties—which continued to be sung until the close of the nineteenth century when sail finally gave place to steam—is about the Black Ball merchant line, notorious for the brutality of its officers:

> Blow[2] the man down, bullies, blow the man down,
> *Way, ay—blow the man down!*

[1] many people   [2] knock

O, blow the man down in Liverpool Town,
Give me some time to blow the man down!

'Twas on a Black Baller I first served my time,
And on that Black Baller I wasted my prime.

'Tis when a Black Baller is clear of the land,
Our boatswain first gives us the word of command.

'Lay aft,' is the cry, 'to the break of the poop,
Or I'll help you along with the toe of my boot!'

Then larboard and starboard on the deck you will sprawl,
For 'Kicking Jack Williams' commands that Black Ball.

'Tis when a Black Baller returns to her dock,
The lassies and lads to the pierhead do flock.

Blow the man down, bullies, blow the man down!
O, blow the man down in Liverpool Town.

As I was walking down Paradise Street,
A brass-bound policeman I happened to meet.

Says he: 'You're a Black-baller by the cut of your hair.
I know you're a Black-baller by the clothes that you wear.'

'O policeman, O policeman, you do me great wrong,
I'm a *Flying Fish* sailor, just home from Hong Kong.'

They gave me three months in Liverpool Town:
For booting and kicking and blowing him down.

The song-leader would improvise new verses about events of the voyage in progress when he remembered no more of the traditional ones.

The Cleveland *Lyke Wake Dirge* (13)—sung when lighting the candles around a corpse and placing a platter of salt on its breast—might, I suppose, be called an occupational ballad. However, most of the other pieces in this collection were solos sung to the harp, to entertain people while eating and drinking, and few of

xiii

them have choruses. They fit the common dictionary definition of the ballad as 'a simple, spirited poem in short stanzas in which some popular story is graphically told'—a definition that can be considerably amplified. These ballads are ascribed to no author; many exist in several different versions; their tunes are almost always in a haunting minor key; they are clearly not the work of either court poets or townsmen; humour is rare; they preach no sermon or political message; they appeal to the heart rather than to the head; most of them concern the twin themes of love and death; and the stories are cut down to the bare bones, with a careful avoidance of rhetoric. A favourite device for holding the audience's attention is to create suspense by arranging incidents in three. Thus the enchanted Isabel gives Kemp Owyne (5) a belt, a ring, and then a sword; and at the third gift he frees her from the spell. Sir Andrew Barton (31) sends first a Gordon, next a Hamilton, to climb the mainmast of his ship and 'let the beams down fall', but finally goes himself and is killed by the last arrow in William Horseley's quiver. In the *Lyke Wake Dirge* (13), the spirit of the dead has to pass over Whinny Muir, across the Brig of Dread, and then face the concluding ordeal of Purgatory fire.

At one time these ballads were the stock-in-trade of, but not necessarily composed by, strolling minstrels such as Sir Walter Scott celebrated:

> The way was long, the wind was cold,
> The minstrel was infirm and old;
> His harp, his sole remaining joy,
> Was carried by an orphan boy.

These minstrels—the word *ministralis* means 'a dependant'—were first kept by great landlords for the entertainment of their households; but the Wars of the Roses, and other troubles, must have sent many of them out to seek their fortunes with harp or viol in the countryside. Some ballads are complete in themselves; some only fragments. It seems that the English minstrel often followed Welsh and Gaelic practice: he told his stories in prose, but every so often, on coming to a dramatic situation where (say) a beautiful woman was deserted or betrayed, or brother killed brother, he reached for the harp and sang the appropriate lament. There is a Scottish ballad of four lines:

> Happy the craw[1]
> That biggs[2] in the Trotten shaw[3]
> And drinks o' the water o' Dye,
> For nae mair may I.

The hero's name has long been forgotten, but he had clearly hoped to win a bride and build a house for her near Dye Water in Kincardineshire, but was mortally wounded in the attempt. Another four-line ballad:

> You and I and Amyas,
>   Amyas and you and I,
> To the greenwood we must go, alas!
>   You and I, my life, and Amyas . . .

has also lost its context. But the lady's lover is evidently going off into the greenwood to fight it out with her husband Amyas, as in *The Dead Brother* (25), while she looks helplessly on.

Then there is:

> O western wind, when wilt thou blow
>   That the small rain down may rain?
> Christ, that my love were in my arms
>   And I in my bed again!

where the speaker has had his true love taken from him by night, and is lying wounded and with a parched throat in open country.

The Unquiet Grave (17), though sometimes found at the end of *Clerk Saunders*, a ballad which tells how the brothers of a certain 'Maid Margret' killed her lover, probably formed part of a lost prose tale.

The subjects of such ballads as *The Demon Lover* (11), *Clerk Colvill* (4), *Kemp Owyne* (5), and *Lord Rendal* (3), are folk tales

---

[1] crow   [2] builds   [3] wood

found in different versions all over Europe and Asia. Others, like *Johnny Faa, the Lord of Little Egypt* (21), *Chevy Chase* (26), *Sir Andrew Barton* (31) and the *Banished Duke of Grantham* (38), record historical or semi-historical events. Occasionally, a story is borrowed from the Gospels, as with *The Cherry Tree Carol* (10); and *Bruton Town* (32) may be a popular version of Boccaccio's story 'The Pot of Basil'.

Frequent traces of the Old Religion are found in the Robin Hood ballads. For instance, the duel between the Robin and the Wren (emblems, respectively, of the Celtic gods Belin and Bran) is the subject of *Robin and Gandelyn* (12), in which Robin Hood, killed by little Wrennock, gets avenged by his 'knave', or New Year successor. 'Robin' was a title often given to the male leader of a witch coven, the female leader being called the 'Maid'—hence 'Maid Marian'. The original character who inspired the legends of Robin Hood is shown by J. W. Walker (*The Yorkshire Archaeological Journal*, 1944) to have been a yeoman of Wakefield in Yorkshire, born about 1285, and outlawed for joining the rebellion of the Earl of Lancaster, whom King Edward II defeated at Boroughbridge in 1322. Robin was the son of a forester named Adam Hood. King Edward, during his northern progress in the following year, seems to have daringly visited the greenwood—he wanted to raise a corps of English archers, trained by Robin Hood, who could avenge his recent defeat by Robert Bruce at Bannockburn. In *The Geste of Robin Hood*, the King grants Robin a free pardon and invites him to London; but, after fifteen months, Robin grows weary of Court life and returns to the greenwood. Mr. Walker shows that the name 'Robin Hood' figures in the register of Court Expenses for the years 1323 and 1324 as the leader of a company of royal archers. Edward II was eventually forced to abdicate; Edward III, however, profited from his father's foresight when, in 1346, the English archers proved their supremacy at Crécy; and again in the following year at Neville's Cross, when they helped him to defeat and capture the King of Scotland.

Later balladists either misunderstood or misrepresented Robin's deep reverence for 'Our Lady'. As we know from the Scottish witch trials, she was not necessarily the Virgin Mary. One such trial in 1597 showed that a certain Marion Grant of Aberdeen, known to her followers as 'the Queen of Elphame', who 'had a grip of all the craft'—that is, controlled the entire Scottish witch cult—also used 'Our Lady' as a title. A thirteenth-century 'Queen of Elphame' occurs in the ballad of *Thomas the Rimer* (6), and another is mentioned at a 1655 witch trial. And though the expression 'to shoot a penny' (*The Death of Robin Hood* 33) is changed in some versions of the Robin Hood ballads to 'shoot for a penny', we learn from a mediaeval treatise on witchcraft— called *Malleus Maleficarum*, or 'Hammer of the Evil Women'— that Continental archers, before being allowed to join the archer guilds, were required to 'shoot in the Devil's name' not only at apples on their children's heads (as William Cloudesley does in an English ballad), but at crosses and crucifixes, to prove their rejection of Christianity. Every silver penny had a cross on the reverse side; being about the size of a sixpence and made of very poor metal, it must have been as difficult a target to hit as a willow wand.

At least fifty different ballads commemorate the deeds of Robin Hood; several of them exist in many variants. On May Day, Midsummer Day and Lammas, the whole Northern countryside gave itself up to festivities in his honour. Preaching before Edward VI, Bishop Latimer complains that:

> . . . I came once myself to a place riding on a journey homeward from London, and I sent word overnight into the town that I would preach there in the morning, because it was a holy day, and methought it was a holy day's work: the church stood in my way, and I took my horse and my company and went thither, I thought I should have found a great company in the church, and when I came there the church door was fast locked. I tarried there half an hour and more, and at last the key was found. And one of the parish comes to me and says: 'Sir, this is a busy day with us; we cannot hear you. It is Robin Hood's Day. The Parish are gone abroad for

Robin Hood, I pray you hinder them not.' I was fain there to give place to Robin Hood. It is no laughing matter, my friends, it is a weeping matter, a heavy matter under the pretence for gathering for Robin Hood, a traitor and a thief, to put out a preacher, to prefer Robin Hood before the ministration of God's word.

In England, strolling minstrels disappeared during Queen Elizabeth's reign; either arrested as 'vagabonds' or put out of date by the spread of town literature and amusements to the country villages—for along with the pedlar and cheap-jack came a new arrival, the ballad-seller. He carried a pack of 'broad-sheets', or 'broadsides'—narrative verses in a more modern and lively style than the countryfolk had hitherto known. Here is a minstrel from Henry Chettle's *King Harte's Dreame*, whose trade has been taken by these newcomers:

> He was an old fellow low of stature: his head was covered with a round cap, his body with a side-skirted tawny coat, his legs and feet trussed up in leather buskins, his grey hairs and furrowed face witnessed his age, his treble-viol in his hand assured me of his profession. On which (by his continual sawing having but one string) he gave me a hunt's-up ... I remembered him to be no other than old Anthony Now-Now.

He complained that 'times are changed, and men are changed in the times'; and that, though one of the few ballad minstrels excepted by Elizabeth's stringent law against able-bodied rogues and vagabonds, he had not benefited in the least. Players and fiddlers were liable under this law to the usual punishment for vagabondage, namely, branding in the ear—unless they could prove that they were employed by a respectable citizen. The pitches being thus cleared of 'masterless men', the respectable London stationers found it profitable to engage apprentices and, instead of teaching them their regular trade, which was to act as bookstall managers, would send them out singing and selling ballads in the neighbouring shires. 'Is it not lamentable that such a flock of runagates should overspread the face of this land, as at this time it doth?' asks Anthony Now-Now. He describes:

... the blushless faces of certain Babies, sons to one Barnes most frequenting Bishop's Stafford ... The one in a queaking treble, the other in an ale-blown bass carol out such ribaldry as chaste ears abhor to hear and modesty hath no tongue to utter ... while the old ale-knight their dad breaks out in admiration and sends straggling customers to admire the roaring of his sons: where ... they hear no better matter than the lascivious under-songs of *Watkin's Ale*, *The Carman's Whistle*, *Chopping Knives* and *Friar Foxtail*, and that with such odious and detested boldness as if there be any one line in those lewd songs than other more abominable, that one with a double repetition is loudly bellowed, as for example of the friar and the nun:

'He whipt her with a fox's tail,' sings Barnes minor.

'And he whipt her with a fox's tail,' sings Barnes major.

'O, brave boys,' said Barnes Maximus. The father leaps, the lubbers roar, the people run, the Devil laughs, God lours, and good men weep.

And here is another burlesqued ballad-seller: Shakespeare's Autolycus of *The Winter's Tale*. His pedlar's licence protected him against the vagabondage laws.

CLOWN: What hast here? ballads?

MOPSA: Pray now, buy some! I love a ballad in print o' life, for then we are sure they are true.

AUTOLYCUS: Here's a ballad of a fish that appeared upon the west on Wednesday the fourscore of April, forty thousand fathom above water and sung this ballad against the hard hearts of maids. It is thought she was a woman and was turned into a cold fish for she would not exchange kisses with one that loved her. The ballad is very pitiful and as true.

DORCAS: Is it true, think you?

AUTOLYCUS: Five justices' hands at it, and witnesses more than my pack will hold.

CLOWN: Lay it by: another!

AUTOLYCUS: This is a passing merry one and goes to the tune of *Two maids wooing a man*. There's scarce a maid westward but she sings it: 'tis in request, I can tell you.

The account is not much exaggerated. A ballad in the Shirburn collection of broadsheets is entitled: '*A most miraculous strange and trewe ballad of a maid now dwelling at the town of Meurs in*

Dutchland, that hath not taken any food this 16 years and is not yet neither hungry nor thirsty: the which maid hath lately been presented to the Lady Elizabeth the King's daughter of England. This song was made by the maid herself and now translated into English.'

Such ballads were, as *The Winter's Tale* quotation shows, set to familiar tunes, not given new ones, which marks an important stage in popular ballad history. The story was getting the upper hand of the music. These broadsheets were, indeed, the chief means of circulating news of national importance or journalistic interest. But Anthony Now-Now was biased in describing all of them as insolently ribald. Many of them expressed deep indignation at the villainies they recorded; and many, like the broadsheet ballad of *The Children in the Wood* (37), the first appearance of *The Babes in the Wood*, were innocency itself. For two centuries after Shakespeare's death the broadside did a good trade: until Dickens' day the walls of inns were regularly papered with them. Newspapers, sold at sixpence or a shilling, offered no competition as yet; the end of the broadside's popularity came with universal education, when penny and halfpenny newspapers could be sold at a profit in country districts.

The minstrels had sung mostly of kings, queens, and the nobility; but there were also numerous ale-house songs, written by men of greater or less education—including King James IV of Scotland (*The Gaberlunzie Man* 34), John Skelton who was Henry VIII's tutor and the leading scholar of his age, and many thieves or rogues. I have included a few specimens here. Some were amorous, some religious, some humorous (*King John and the Abbot* 22; *Get Up and Bar the Door* 23), some nonsensical, some obscene. Most of the new broadsheet ballads followed the ale-house tradition; but few proved worth memorising, and none came with their own tunes—the broadsheet always advertised: 'To the tune of *Greensleeves*', or 'To the tune of *Cuckolds All A Row*', etc. The haunting and savage melancholy of the minstrel ballad had all but disappeared; it comes as a surprise to find a broadsheet of Charles I's time with so old-fashioned a chorus as:

> Cold, cold and wondrous cold,
> And through the bush the wind blows cold . . .

The stationer's apprentice not only sang his ballads at the fairs: he sometimes acted them, and often enough two or more performers took part. Favourite subjects were quarrels between a husband and his wife; or between a virtuous girl and her wicked tempter. Accounts of murders and other violent crimes were the best 'get-pennies' (money-makers), as they are today, but it was common practice to add a moral warning—such as that innocent girls should not speak to handsome strangers, nor honest citizens go unarmed across Hounslow Heath. Monstrous births—two-faced children, or pigs with dolphin heads—were also popular subjects:

> What might these monsters to us teach,
>   Which now are sent so rife,
> But that we have God's word well preached
>   And will not mend our life?

Four ballads were published to celebrate the defeat of the Spanish Armada in 1588; and two about the burning of Beccles, a Suffolk town, in 1586; the several conspiracies against Queen Elizabeth produced a crop of loyal 'Warnings to All False Traitors'; and in 1570, Pope Pius V was mocked in another group of ballads for excommunicating her. However, the censorship was strong and no ballads were licensed about the Earl of Essex (whom she loved but was forced to execute for rebellion) until after her death two years later.

When news (true or false) failed, ballads were published about ancient events in English history, about the Trojan War, about King Arthur and his Knights, about the Wandering Jew, about Tom Thumb, about Guy of Warwick. The Robin Hood cycle was enlarged, and a rival archer, Adam Bell, introduced to an eager public. Then the Puritans, thinking it wrong that the Devil should have all the best tunes, re-wrote popular love-songs, giving them a religious twist. Thus:

> Row well, ye mariners . .

became:

> Row well, God's mariners . . .

and:

> Dainty, come thou to me!

became:

> Jesus, come thou to me!

The Puritans also condemned ballads that seemed to threaten the country's morals, and often succeeded in having the printers fined. Revenge on private enemies was sometimes taken by publishing scurrilous ballads about them. Thus in Shakespeare's *Henry IV*, Falstaff threatens vengeance on Prince Hal and his friends, for the tricks they are playing on him, by having 'ballads made on you all, sung to filthy tunes'. And in *Antony and Cleopatra*, the Queen and her maids of honour are terrified by the fear of ballad publicity.

Politics made a strong intrusion into broadsheet literature at the time of the Civil Wars; and in the eighteenth century, Whigs and Tories both realised the electioneering value of satiric ballads, and roared them lustily in mug-houses and gentlemen's clubs. Proceedings at these sing-songs were regulated by a president, who sat in an arm-chair, some steps above the company, to keep order. In *The Club Room*, we see this personage at work:

> In my club room so great,
> When I'm seated in state,
> At the head of the table I shine.
> With hammer in hand,
> Zounds! how I command
> As I push round the bumpers of wine.
> Then after we've toasted the health of the King,
> Mr. Briscket the butcher is called on to sing . . .

Mr. Briscket sang, and seems to have frequently finished his song underneath the table. The broadsheet ballad was not, however, always propagandist or journalistic: often the stationer-printers, whom Anthony Now-Now described as 'Devil's Instruments, intruders into Printing's mystery, by whom that excellent Art is not smally slandered, the Government of the Estate not a little blemished, nor Religion in the least measure hindered', struck off pirated versions of his own ballads for the convenience of districts where they had not yet penetrated. Though these versions are sometimes 'improved' by a thorough smoothing out of the metre, more 'poetical' diction, and a modernisation of the story to make it acceptable as a news item, this is not invariably the case; a printer often found it easier to record what he heard.

In Scotland, new minstrel ballads continued to appear until the late seventeenth century. This was no longer the case in the English countryside, although rousing songs, such as *Admiral Benbow* (35), were sung in the Navy; and something of the old Robin Hood spirit reappeared in a group of ballads composed by criminals and their associates, the heroes being murderers who defied law and order to the last—for example, *Sam Hall*, an early version of which provided *Admiral Benbow* with its tune. Sam Hall declares that 'I hate you one and all', and even curses the Judge before whom he is being tried for his life:

> O, his Lordship he did stare,
>   G——m his eyes,
> O, his Lordship he did stare,
>   G——m his eyes,
> O, his Lordship he did stare
> For to hear me curse and swear,
> For to hear me curse and swear,
>   G——m his eyes!
>
> There was Molly in the crowd,
>   G——m her eyes,
> There was Molly in the crowd,
>   G——m her eyes,
> There was Molly in the crowd,
> And says I to her out loud:
> 'Why, Molly, ain't you proud?
>   G——m your eyes!'

Sam Hall went cursing and unrepentant to the gallows, spurning all attempts of the Methodist minister to save his soul. Other heroes of this sort were 'Poor Little Jimmy Murphy', for whom the ladies wept pityingly; and Larry, who showed memorable courage on the night before he was hanged, and when a priest came to confess him 'pitched his big wig to the Devil'. Towards the end of this collection I print *Wednesbury Cocking* (36), which proves that the spirit of old Anthony Now-Now, driven underground by Elizabethan penal laws, the Civil Wars, and Methodism, enjoyed a strange new flowering in the gin shops and cockpits of the eighteenth and early nineteenth centuries.

Nevertheless, the old minstrel ballads continued until a few years ago to be sung in the chimney corners of English and Scottish farmhouses, as also in the hills of Virginia, Kentucky and Tennessee, where seventeenth-century settlers had taken them: always with the same preference, noted by Wordsworth in his *Reaper Lass*, for tales

> ... of old, unhappy, far-off things
> And battles long ago ...

However, the radio, the cinema, and television have killed all that.

Most ballad anthologies published nowadays are 'scholarly', which means that the editors feel obliged to print each ballad exactly as it occurs in one of the many variant versions still surviving. But, unless such a version happens to be superior to all others in every stanza, this seems unjust to the reader, who is entitled to see the best text. Usually, therefore, I have combined several versions, choosing the most telling stanzas, or phrases, from each; and where all versions are obviously defective at some point or other, owing to the mutilation of a manuscript, or the poor memory of singers, I have restored the missing lines in the spirit of the original. Thus, in *Johnny Faa, the Lord of Little Egypt* (21), Johnny's orders for Lady Cassilis to carry him on her back over the lake have dropped out; and in *The Death of Robin Hood*

(33) the old woman's reason for cursing Robin, and the identity of the women who bewail his death, are also missing. Ballad composers seem to have been careful of their rhymes; if an impossibly matched pair occurs in a broadsheet text, one must suppose either that a singer forgot his lines, or that a stationer found one of the rhyming words out of date and meaningless and amended it. To restore the original rhyme from a knowledge of ballad-English is never difficult; and I have done so here and there in *Sir Andrew Barton* and *Admiral Benbow*. One worn-down stanza of the latter runs:

> So the *Ruby* and Benbow
>   Fought the French, fought the French,
> The *Ruby* and Benbow
>   Fought the French,
> They fought them up and down
> Till the blood came trickling down,
> Till the blood came trickling down
>   Where they lay, where they lay . . .

But Benbow's ship was not the *Ruby*; *French* (judging from the other stanzas) ought to rhyme with *lay*; and the fifth, sixth, and seventh lines ought to end in three different rhyming words. All this invites commonsense emendation:

> So brave Benbow sailed alone
>   On that day, on that day,
> Alone against the French,
>   Where they lay.
> He fought them with a frown,
> Till the blood came trickling down—
> And he earned a great renown
>   On that day, on that day.

Ballads are nobody's property, and if careless singers or illiterate printers have claimed the right to spoil them, who can deny us the right to guess how the originals went? Not even the scholars—though they seldom risk a guess themselves. I have modernised the spelling of words in the older ballads wherever this was possible without spoiling the rhyme or breaking the rhythm; there is little virtue in spelling 'dun doe' as 'dandoo'; or 'Go, fetch me down this false bishop' as 'Goe, ffeitch mee doune thysse ffauss bysshoppe.'

R. G.

Deyá,
    Majorca,
        Spain.

BALLADS

The False Knight on the Road

1

'O where are you going?'
  Quoth the false knight on the road.
'I'm going to the school,'
  Quoth the wee boy, and still he stood.

2

'What's that upon your back?'
  Quoth the false knight on the road.
'Wot well it is my books,'
  Quoth the wee boy, and still he stood.

3

'What's that upon your arm?'
  Quoth the false knight on the road.
'Wot well it is my peat,'
  Quoth the wee boy, and still he stood.

4

'Who owns they sheep?'
  Quoth the false knight on the road.
'They are mine and my mother's,'
  Quoth the wee boy, and still he stood.

5

'How many of them are mine?'
  Quoth the false knight on the road.
'All they that have blue tails,'
  Quoth the wee boy, and still he stood.

6

'I wish you were on yonder tree,'
  Quoth the false knight on the road.
'And a good ladder under me,'
  Quoth the wee boy, and still he stood.

7

'And the ladder for to break,'
  Quoth the false knight on the road.
'And you for to fall down,'
  Quoth the wee boy, and still he stood.

8

'I wish you were in yonder sea,'
  Quoth the false knight on the road.
'And a good bottom[1] under me,'
  Quoth the wee boy, and still he stood.

9

'And the bottom for to break,'
  Quoth the false knight on the road.
'And you to be drowned,'
  Quoth the wee boy, and still he stood.

[1] ship

The Twa Sisters of Binnorie

1

There were twa sisters sat in a bower,
  Edinbro', Edinbro',
There came a knight to be their wooer.
  Stirling for aye!
He courted the elder with glove and ring,
But he loved the younger beyond all thing.
  Bonny St. Johnstone stands on Tay.

2

He courted the elder with glove and ring,
But he loved the younger beyond all thing;
He courted the elder with brooch and knife,
But he loved the younger as his life.

3

The elder she was vexéd sair[1]
And sair envied her sister fair.
'O sister, come to the river-strand
And watch the boats as they row to land.'

4

She's ta'en her by the milk-white hand
And led her down to the river strand;
The younger she stood on a stane
And the elder sister threw her in.

[1] sore

5

'O sister, sister, give me your hand
And I'll make you heir to all my land;
O sister, sister, save my life
And I swear I'll never be no man's wife.'

6

'Foul fall the hand that I should take—
It twined me out[1] of my wardle's make[2].
Your cherry cheeks and your yellow hair
Make me go maiden for evermair.'

7

Sometimes she sank, sometimes she swam,
Until she came to the miller's dam;
'O draw the dam,' cried the miller's son,
'Here's either a mermaid or a swan.'

8

The miller quickly focht[3] his dam
And there he found a drowned womán;
You could not see her fingers white,
For golden rings that were so gryte[4].

9

Then by there came a harper fine
Such as harp to nobles when they dine.
He's ta'en three strands of her yellow hair
And with them strung his harp so rare.

10

He's done him[5] to her father's hall
And played the harp before them all.
O then, the harp began to sing,
And it's 'farewell, sweetheart,' sang the string.

[1] it robbed me   [2] my earthly mate   [3] emptied   [4] great   [5] gone

II

And syne[1] the harp spake loud and clear,
    Edinbro', Edinbro',
'Farewell, my father and mother dear!'
    Stirling for aye!
And then as plain as plain could be:
'There sits my sister who drownéd me.'
    Bonny St. Johnstone stands on Tay.

(3)

Lord Rendal

1

'O where have you been, Lord Rendal my son,
O where have you been, my jolly young man?'
'In yonder wild woods, mother; make my bed soon,
For I'm wearied with hunting and fain would lie down.'

2

'And whom met you there, Lord Rendal my son,
And whom met you there, my jolly young man?'
'I met with my true love, mother; make my bed soon,
For I'm wearied with hunting and fain would lie down.'

3

'What got you for dinner, Lord Rendal my son,
What got you for dinner, my jolly young man?'
'A dish of small fishes, mother; make my bed soon,
For I'm wearied with hunting and fain would lie down.'

[1] soon

'What like were the fishes, Lord Rendal my son,
What like were the fishes, my jolly young man?'
'Black backs and speckled bellies: make my bed soon,
For I'm wearied with hunting and fain would lie down.'

'Who got the leavings, Lord Rendal my son,
Who got the leavings, my jolly young man?'
'My hawks and my hounds, mother; make my bed soon,
For I'm wearied with hunting and fain would lie down.'

'And what became of them, Lord Rendal my son,
And what became of them, my jolly young man?'
'They swelled and died, mother; make my bed soon,
For I'm wearied with hunting and fain would lie down.'

'I fear you are poisoned, Lord Rendal my son,
I fear you are poisoned, my jolly young man.'
'O yes I am dying, mother; make my bed soon,
For I'm wearied with hunting and fain would lie down.'

'What will you leave to your mother, Lord Rendal my son,
What will you leave to your mother, my jolly young man?'
'Four and twenty milch-kine, mother; make my bed soon,
For I'm wearied with hunting and fain would lie down.'

'What will you leave to your father, Lord Rendal my son,
What will you leave to your father, my jolly young man?'
'My horse and the saddle, mother; make my bed soon,
For I'm wearied with hunting and fain would lie down.'

'What will you leave to your sister, Lord Rendal my son,
What will you leave to your sister, my jolly young man?'
'Both my gold box and rings, mother; make my bed soon,
For I'm wearied with hunting and fain would lie down.'

11

'What will you leave to your true love, Lord Rendal my son,
What will you leave to your true love, my jolly young man?'
'The tow and the halter[1], mother; make my bed soon,
For I'm wearied with hunting and fain would lie down.'

(4)

Clerk Colvill

1

Clerk[2] Colvill and his lusty[3] dame
   Were walking in the garden green;
The belt around her middle[4] gimp[5]
   Cost Clerk Colvill of crowns fifteen.

2

'O hearken well now, my good lord,
   O hearken well to what I say:
When ye gang by the wells of Slane
   O gang not near the well-fau'rd may[6].'

3

'Now hold your tongue, my lusty dame,
   Now speak nae more of that to me,
For never I saw a fair womán
   That I did like sae well as thee.'

---

[1] a rope to hang her with   [2] an educated man   [3] healthy
[4] waist   [5] slender   [6] the well-favoured, or beautiful, maiden

4

He's mounted on his berry-brown steed,
    Nought minding what his dame had said,
And he's rade by the wells of Slane
    Where washing was a bonny maid.

5

'Wash on, wash on, my bonny maid,
    That wash sae well your sark[1] of silk.'
'It's all for you, my gentle knight,
    My body whiter than the milk.'

6

He's lighted[2] from his berry-brown steed,
    And ta'en her by the sleeve so green,
And he has forgotten his lusty dame
    To gang and kiss with the maid of Slane.

*   *   *

7

Then loud, loud cried the Clerk Colvíll,
    'Ochone, my head it pains me sair!'
'Then take this little pen-knife,' she said,
    'Gin from my sark you'll cut a gare[3],
I'll row[4] it about your lovely head
    And pain you'll never feel nae mair.'

8

O he has taken her little bane-knife[5]
    And from her sark he's cut a gare;
She's rowed it about his whey-white face,
    But aye his head it achéd mair.

[1] bodice   [2] alighted   [3] a strip for a bandage   [4] tie   [5] death knife

'Ochone alas,' cried the Clerk Colvíll,
  'O sairer, sairer aches my head.'
And merrily laughs the maid of Slane:
  'It will aye be worse till ye be dead.'

10

'Will ye lie there,' cried the maid of Slane,
  'Clerk Colvill, till at last ye dee,
Or will ye turn to an otter brown,
  In Clyde watér to sport with me?'

11

'Nay, I'll not sport in Clyde watér,
  I would rather get me hame to dee,
But in spite of all the devils in hell
  With my bright sword I shall first kill thee.'

12

Clerk Colvill drew his grounden glave[1]
  And thought to stick her where she stood
But she was vanished to a fish
  And merrily sprang intil the flood[2].

13

He's mounted on his berry-brown steed
  And dowy[3] dowy rade he hame,
And heavily, heavily lighted down
  When to his lady's bower he came.

14

'O mother, mother, make my bed;
  My gentle lady, lay me down;
And brother, brother, unbend my bow,
  For now I shall not bend it soon.'

[1] sharpened sword   [2] water   [3] doleful

His mother has made Clerk Colvill's bed;
  His lady's on the bed him lain;
His brother he has unbent the bow
  That never was bent by him again.

(5)

Kemp Owyne

1

Her mother died when she was young,
  Which gave her cause to make great moan;
Her father married the worst woman
  That ever lived in Christendom.

2

She servéd her with foot and hand,
  In everything that she could dee[1],
Till once, in an unlucky time,
  She threw her in ower Craigy's sea.

3

Says, 'Lie you there, dove Isabel,
  And all my sorrows lie with thee;
Till Kemp Owyne come ower the sea,
  And borrow[2] you with kisses three,
Let all the world do what they will,
  O borrowed shall you never be!'

4

Her breath grew strang, her hair grew lang,
  And twisted thrice about the tree,
And all the people, far and near,
  Thought that a savage beast was she.

[1] do   [2] ransom

5

These news did come to Kemp Owyne,
  He hasted him to Craigy's sea,
And daunting not to stand him nigh,
  Upon the savage beast looked he.

6

Her breath was strang, her hair was lang,
  And twisted was about the tree,
And with a swing she came about:
  'Come to Craigy's sea, and kiss with me.'

7

'Here is a royal belt,' she cried,
  'That I have found in the green sea;
And while your body it is on,
  Drawn shall your blood never be;
But if you touch me, tail or fin,
  I vow my belt your death shall be.'

8

He steppéd in, gave her a kiss,
  The royal belt he brought him wi';
Her breath was strang, her hair was lang,
  And twisted twice about the tree,
And with a swing she came about:
  'Come to Craigy's sea, and kiss with me.'

9

'Here is a royal ring,' she said,
  'That I have found in yon green sea;
And while your finger it is on,
  Drawn shall your blood never be;
But if you touch me, tail or fin,
  I swear my ring your death shall be.'

He steppéd in, gave her a kiss,
   The royal ring he brought him wi';
Her breath was strang, her hair was lang,
   And twisted once about the tree,
And with a swing she came about:
   'Come to Craigy's sea, and kiss with me.'

'Here is a royal brand,' she said,
   'That I have found in yon green sea;
And while your body it is on,
   Drawn shall your blood never be;
But if you touch me, tail or fin,
   I swear my brand your death shall be.'

He steppéd in, gave her a kiss,
   The royal brand he brought him wi';
Her breath was sweet, her hair grew short,
   And twisted nane about the tree,
And smilingly she came about,
   As fair a woman as fair could be.

'O was it wolf into[1] the wood,
   Or was it fish into the sea,
Or was it man, or wily woman,
   My true love, that misshapit thee?'

'It was no wolf into the wood,
   Nor was it fish into the sea,
But it was my false stepmothér,
   O woe an weary might she be!

[1] within

'O a heavier weird[1] light her upon
Than ever fell on false womán;
May her hair grow rough, and her teeth grow lang,
And on her four feet may she gang,
May none take pity her upon,
But in Wormie's Wood she shall aye wone[2].'

(6)

Thomas the Rimer

1

Thomas lay on the Huntlie bank,
  A-spying ferlies[3] with his ee,
And he did espy a lady bold
  Come riding down from the eldern tree.

2

Her skirt was of the grass-green silk,
  Her mantle of the velvet fine,
Her steed was of the dapple-grey,
  And at its mane there hung bells nine.
Her hawk and hounds she had her with,
  And her bugle horn with gold did shine.

3

Thomas took off both cloak and cap,
  And bowed him low down till the knee.
'O save you, save you, Queen of Heaven,
  For your peer on earth I ne'er did see!'

---

[1] fate   [2] live   [3] wonders   [4] elder

4

'I'm not the Queen of Heaven, Thomas,
  That name does not belong to me;
I am but the Queen of fair Elphame
  Come out to hunt in my follie.

5

'Now gin[1] ye kiss my mouth, Thomás,
  Ye must not miss my fair bodie;
Then ye may e'en gae hame and tell
  That ye have lain with a gay ladie.'

6

'O gin I love a lady fair,
  No ill tales of her would I tell;
And it is with thee I fain would gae
  Though it were e'en to Heaven or Hell.'

7

'Then harp and carp[2], Thomás,' she said.
  'Then harp and carp along with me,
But it will be seven years and a day
  Till ye win back to your ain countrie.'

8

She turned about her milk-white steed
  True Thomas followed her behind,
And aye whene'er her bridle rang
  The steed flew swifter than the wind.

9

It was dark night and no star light,
  The lady rade, True Thomas ran,
And ever again he heard her bells,
  Until he came to a water wan.

[1] if   [2] talk

Thorough that water the lady went,
   And Thomas waded above the knee,
There he saw neither sun nor moon,
   But he heard the roaring of the sea.

Then they rade on and farther on,
   Until they came to a garden green;
'Light down, light down, let me pull an apple'—
   For lack of food he was like to tyne[1].

'O hold your hand, True Thomas,' she cried,
   'That apple must not be touched by thee.
For all the plagues that are in hell
   Light on the fruit of this countrie.

'But I have a loaf here in my lap,
   Likewise a bottle of good red wine.
And now ere we gae farther on
   We will rest awhile, and ye may dine.

'And when ye've eaten and drunk your fill
   Lay down your head upon my knee;
Then will I take you to yon green hill
   And there I'll show you ferlies three.

Thomas has eaten and drunk his fill,
   And laid his head on the lady's knee,
And she's taken him to thon green hill
   And from it showed him ferlies three.

[1] die

'O see not ye yon narrow road,
　　So thick beset with thorns and briars?
That is the path of righteousness,
　　Though after it but few enquiries.

17

'And see not ye that broad, broad road
　　That lies across yon lily leven[1]?
That is the path of wickedness,
　　Though some call it the road to Heaven.

18

'And see not ye that bonny road
　　That winds about the ferny brae[2]?
That is the road to fair Elphame
　　Where you and I this night must gae.

19

'And when ye come to our Court, Thomás,
　　See that a well-learned man ye be,
For they will ask ye, one and all,
　　And ye must answer none but me.

20

'Then I will answer them again
　　That I got your oath at the eldern tree,
But gin one word ye should chance to speak
　　You will ne'er win back to your ain countrie.

[1] lawn　　　　[2] hillside

'For ilka¹ seven years, True Thomas,
    We pay our teindings² unto hell,
And ye're so leesome³ and so strong
    That I fear, Thomas, it will be yoursel'.'

*   *   *

22

He's gotten a coat of the even⁴ cloth
    And a pair of shoes of velvet green,
And till seven years were past and gone
    True Thomas on earth was never seen.

(7)

Sir Patrick Spens

1

The King sits in Dumfermlin town
    Drinking the blood-red wine:
'O, where will I get a skilly⁵ skipper
    Will sail this good ship of mine?'

2

Then up and spake an eldern knight
    Sat at the King's right knee:
'Sir Patrick Spens is the best sailór
    That ever sailed the sea.'

¹ every   ² tithes   ³ loveable   ⁴ smooth   ⁵ skilful

3

The King has written a broad lettér
  And sealed it with his hand,
And sent it to Sir Patrick Spens
  Was walking on the strand.

4

'O who is the man has done this deed,
  This ill deed done to me?
To send me out this time of the year
  To sail upon the sea?

5

'To Norraway, to Norraway,
  To Norraway o'er the faem.
The King's daughter of Norraway,
  'Tis I must bring her hame.'

6

They have mounted sail on a Monday morn
  With all the haste they may,
And they have landed in Norraway
  Upon the Wednesday.

7

They had not been a week, a week
  In Norraway but three,
Till lords of Norraway gan to say
  'Ye spend all our white monie[1].

8

'Ye spend all our good kingis gold
  But and[2] our queenis fee[3].'
'Ye lie, ye lie, ye liars loud:
  Full loud I hear you lie.

---

[1] silver   [2] also   [3] dowry

18

9

'For I have brought as much white monie
   As will gain[1] my men and me.
I have brought a half-fou[2] of good red gold
   Out o'er the sea with me.

10

'Be it wind or weet, be it snow or sleet
   Our ships must sail the morn.'
'O ever alack my master dear,
   I fear a deadly storm.

11

'I saw the new moon late yestreen
   With the old moon in her arm.
And if we go to sea, mastér,
   I fear we'll come to harm.'

12

They had not sailed a league, a league,
   A league but barely three,
Came wind and weet and snow and sleet
   And gurly[3] grew the sea.

13

'O where will I get a pretty boy
   Will take my steer in hand,
Till I get up to the tall topmast
   To see if I can spy land?'

14

He had not gone a step, a step,
   A step but barely ane,
When a bolt flew out of the good ship's side,
   And the salt sea it came in.

---

[1] serve   [2] half-bushel   [3] rough

15

Come back, come back, my pretty boy,
　　Lest you should come to harm.
For the salt sea's in at our coat neck,
　　And out at the left arm.

16

They fetcht a web of the silken cloth,
　　Another of the twine.
They wapped[1] them round the good ship's side,
　　And still the sea came in.

17

Loth, loth, were our Scottish lords
　　To wet their cork-heeled shoon,
But yet ere all the play was played
　　Their hats were wet aboon[2].

18

O lang, lang may their ladies sit
　　With their fans into their hand,
Or ever they see Sir Patrick Spens
　　Come sailing to the land.

19

O lang, lang may the ladies stand
　　With their gold combs in their hair
All waiting for their own dear lords
　　That they shall not see mair.

20

There was Saturday and Sabbath-day,
　　And Monnynday at morn,
Then featherbeds and silken sheets
　　Come floating to Kinghorn.

[1] swathed　　　[2] above

Half owre, half owre to Aberdour
  'Tis fifty fathoms deep,
And there lies good Sir Patrick Spens
  With the Scots lords at his feet.

(8)

The Twa Corbies[1]

I

As I was walking all alone,
Down a down a down hey down
I heard twa corbies making a moan:
The one unto the other say,
'Where shall we gang and dine today?'
With a down, derry, derry, derry down.

2

'In behind yon auld fail[2] dyke
I wot there lies a new slain knight;
And nobody kens that he lies there,
But his hawk, his hound, and his lady fair.

3

'His hound is to the hunting gane,
His hawk to fetch the wild-fowl hame,
His lady's ta'en another mate,
So we may make our dinner sweet.

---

[1] crows   [2] turf

4

'Ye'll sit on his white hause-bane[1],
And I'll pike out his bonny blue een;
And with one lock of his golden hair
We'll theek[2] our nest when it grows bare.

5

'Many a one for him makes moan,
Down a down a down hey down.
But none shall ken where he is gone;
O'er his white banes, when they are bare,
The wind shall blow for evermair.'
With a down, derry, derry, derry down.

(9)

Hugh of Lincoln

1

Four and twenty bonny boys
   Were playing at the ball,
And by it came him, sweet Sir Hugh,
   And he played o'er them all.

2

He kicked the ball with his right foot,
   And catched it with his knee,
And through and through the Jew's window
   He gared[3] the bonny ball flee.

---

[1] neckbone   [2] line   [3] made

3

He's done him[1] to the Jew's castéll,
    And walked it round about;
And there he saw the Jew's daughtér,
    At the window looking out.

4

'Throw down the ball, ye Jew's daughtér,
    Throw down the ball to me!'
'Never a bit,' says the Jew's daughtér,
    'Till up to me come ye.'

5

'How will I come up? How can I come up?
    How can I come to thee?
For as ye did to my old fathér,
    The same ye'll do to me.'

6

She's gone until her father's garden,
    For an apple red and green;
'Twas all to wile him, sweet Sir Hugh,
    And to entice him in.

7

She's led him in through one dark door,
    And so has she through nine;
She's laid him on a dressing-table,
    And stickit him like a swine.

8

And first came out the thick, thick blood,
    And syne[2] came out the thin,
And syne came out the bonny heart's blood;
    There was no more within.

[1] gone   [2] next

She's rowed[1] him in a cake of lead,
    Bade him lie still and sleep;
She's thrown him in Our Lady's draw-well,
    Was fifty fathom deep.

10

The bells were rung, and mass was sung,
    And all the bairns came home;
When every lady got home her son,
    The Lady Maisry got none.

11

She's ta'en her mantle her about,
    Her coffer by the hand,
And she's gone out to seek her son,
    And wander'd o'er the land.

12

She's done her to the Jew's castéll,
    Where all were fast asleep:
'Gin ye be there, my sweet Sir Hugh,
    I pray you to me speak.'

13

She's done her to the Jew's gardén,
    Thought he had been gathering fruit:
'Gin ye be there, my sweet Sir Hugh,
    I pray you to me bruit[2].'

14

She's near'd Our Lady's deep draw-well,
    Was fifty fathom deep:
'Where'er ye be, my sweet Sir Hugh,
    I pray you to me speak.'

[1] rolled, or wrapped   [2] make a noise

'Go home, go home, my mother dear,
  Prepare my winding sheet,
And at the back of merry Lincoln
  The morn[1] I will you meet.'

Now Lady Maisry is gone home,
  Made him a winding sheet,
And at the back of merry Lincoln
  The dead corpse did her meet.

And all the bells of merry Lincoln
  Without men's hands were rung,
And all the books of merry Lincoln
  Were read without man's tongue,
And ne'er was such a burial
  Since Adam's days begun.

(10)

The Cherry Tree Carol

1

Joseph was an old man
  And an old man was he,
When he married Maid Mary
  The Queen of Galilee.

[1] tomorrow

2

Joseph and Mary walkéd
   Through an orchard green,
Where was berries and cherries
   As thick as might be seen.

3

O then bespoke Mary
   So meek and so mild,
'Pluck me a cherry, Joseph,
   For I am with child.'

4

O then bespoke Joseph
   So wilful and wild,
'Let him pluck thee cherries
   That got thee with child.'

5

O then bespoke the Babe
   Within his mother's womb,
'Bow down, then, the tallest tree,
   For my mother to have some.'

6

Then bowed down the tallest tree
   Unto his mother's hand;
Then she cried: 'See, Joseph,
   I have cherries at command!'

7

As Joseph was a-walking
   He heard angels sing:
'This night shall be born to us
   Our heavenly king.

8

'He neither shall be born to us
  In house nor in hall,
Nor in the place of Paradise,
  But in an ox's stall.

9

'He neither shall be clothéd
  In purple nor in pall,
But all in fair linen
  Such as wear babies all.

10

'He neither shall be rockéd
  In silver nor in gold
But all in a wooden cradle
  That stands on the mould.'

11

Then Mary took her babe
  Up on her left knee:
With 'Dear child, I pray thee now,
  Tell how this world shall be.'

12

'On the fifth day of January
  Three kings shall draw near,
While the stars in the Heaven
  Do tremble for fear.

13

'Upon the Good Friday
  I will hang on a rood
And all the seed of Adam
  I'll buy with my blood.

14

'For I shall be so dead, Mother,
  As the stones in the wall:
O the stones in the street, Mother,
  Shall mourn for me all.

15

'Upon Easter Day, Mother,
  My rising shall be:
O, the sun and the moon then
  Shall uprise with me.'

(11)

The Demon Lover

1

'O where have you been, my dear, dear love,
  This long seven years and more?'
'O I'm come to seek my former vows
  Ye granted me before.'

2

'O hold your tongue of your former vows,
  For they will breed sad strife;
O hold your tongue of your former vows,
  For I am become a wife.'

3

He turned him right and round about,
  And the tear blinded his ee;
'I would never have trodden on Irish ground,
  If it had not been for thee.

4

'I might have had a king's daughtér,
    Far, far beyond the sea;
I might have had a king's daughtér,
    Were it not for love of thee.'

5

'If ye might have had a king's daughtér,
    Yourself ye had to blame;
Ye might have taken the king's daughtér,
    For ye kenned that I was nane[1].

6

'If I were to leave my husband dear,
    And my two babes also,
O what have you to take me to,
    If with you I should go?'

7

'I have seven ships upon the sea,
    The eighth brought me to land;
With four and twenty bold mariners.
    And music on every hand.'

8

She has taken up her two little babes,
    Kissed them both cheek and chin;
'O fare ye well, my own two babes,
    For I'll never see you again.'

9

She set her foot upon the ship,
    No mariners could she behold;
But the sails were of the taffety,
    And the masts of the beaten gold.

[1] none

She had not sailed a league, a league,
 A league but barely three,
When dismal grew his countenance,
 And drumlie¹ grew his ee.

They had not sailed a league, a league,
 A league but barely three,
Until she espied his cloven foot,
 And she wept right bitterly.

'O hold your tongue of your weeping,' says he,
 'Of your weeping now let me be;
I will show you how the lilies grow
 On the banks of Italy.'

'O what hills are they, those pleasant hills,
 That the sun shines sweetly on?'
'O those are the hills of Heaven,' he said,
 'Where you shall never wone².'

'O whaten³ a mountain is that,' she said,
 'So dreary with frost and snow?'
'O that is the mountain of Hell,' he cried,
 'Where you and I must go.'

He struck the top-mast with his hand,
 The fore-mast with his knee;
And he brake that gallant ship in twain,
 And sank her in the sea.

¹ gloomy ² live ³ what kind of

(12)

Robin and Gandelyn

1

I heard the carping[1] of a clerk[2]
    All at yon woodë's end—
Of good Robín and Gandelyn
    Was there no other send.[3]
Robin lyeth in greenwood bounden.

2

Strong thievës were those children[4] none,
    But bowmen good and hend[5];
They went to wood to get them flesh
    If God would it them send.

3

All day went out those children two,
    And flesh they could find none
Until again it were evening;
    And then they would go home.

4

Half a hundred of fat fallow deer
    These two did come upon,
And all were fair and fat enough,
    But markéd were by none.
'By my dear God,' said good Robín,
    'Hereof we shall have one!'

[1] talking   [2] educated man   [3] message   [4] young noblemen   [5] handy

5

Robin bent his jolly bow,
  Therein he set a flo[1],
And of the fattest deer of all
  The heart he cleft in two.

6

He haddë not the deer y-flayed,
  Nor half out of the hide,
Ere came a shrewd arrow out of the west
  That felléd[2] Robin's pride.

7

Gandelyn lookéd him east and west,
  By every side with drede[3].
'Who hath my master slain?' he saith,
  'And who hath done this deed?
I shall never out of greenwood go
  Till I see his sidës bleed!'

8

Gandelyn lookéd him east and west,
  And sought under the sun,
And lo, he saw a little boy
  Was clepen[4] Wrennock of Dun.

9

He had a good bow in his hand,
  An arrow to his thumb,
And four and twenty arrows more
  All trusséd[5] in a thrum[6].
'O ware thee, ware thee, Gandelyn!
  Hereof thou shalt have some.

[1] arrow   [2] killed   [3] dread
[4] called   [5] tied   [6] bundle

'O ware thee, ware thee, Gandelyn,
  Hereof thou gyst[1] plentie.'
'Ever one for another,' said Gandelyn,
  'Misaunter[2] have he would flee.'

11

'O where now shall our markë be?'
  Bespoke bold Gandelyn.
'Each one at the other's heart,'
  Wrennock answered again.

12

Wrennock shot a full good shot,
  And he shot none too high—
Thoróugh the sanchothis of his breek[3];
  It touchéd neither thigh.

13

'Now hast thou given me one before,'
  All thus to Wrennock said he,
'But through the might of Our Lady now
  A better I shall give thee.'

14

Gandelyn bent his good yew bow
  And set therein a flo,
He shot thoróugh the green kirtýl[4]:
  His heart he cleft in two.

15

'Now shalt thou never yelp, Wrennóck,
  At alë nor at wine:
That thou hast slain both good Robín
  And his knave[5] Gandelyn.

[1] gettest   [2] Mischance fall on him who avoids the conflict
[3] the fork of his breeches   [4] an upper garment   [5] servant

16

'Now shalt thou never yelp, Wrennóck,
　At winë nor at ale:
That thou hast slain both good Robín
　And Gandelyn of the Dale.'
Robin lyeth in greenwood bounden.

(13)

The Cleveland Lyke Wake[1] Dirge

1

This ae[2] night, this ae night,
　Every night and all;
Fire and selte[3] and candle-light;
　And Christ receive thy saule.

2

When thou from hence away are passed,
　Every night and all,
To Whinny-muir thou comest at last;
　And Christ receive thy saule.

3

If ever thou gavest hosen and shoon,
　Every night and all,
Sit thee down and put them on;
　And Christ receive thy saule.

4

If hosen and shoon thou ne'er gavest nane,
　Every night and all,
The whins shall pyke[4] thee to the bare bane;
　And Christ receive thy saule.

---

[1] corpse-watch　　　[2] one　　　[3] salt　　　[4] pierce

5

From Whinny-muir when thou mayest pass,
Every night and all,
To Brig[1] of Dread thou comest at last;
And Christ receive thy saule.

6

If ever thou gave of thy silver and gold,
Every night and all,
At Brig of Dread thou'lt find foothold;
And Christ receive thy saule.

7

If silver or gold thou ne'er gavest nane,
Every night and all,
Thou'lt tumble down towards hell's flame;
And Christ receive thy saule.

8

From Brig of Dread when thou mayest pass,
Every night and all,
To Purgatory fire thou comest at last;
And Christ receive thy saule.

9

If ever thou gavest meat or drink,
Every night and all,
The fire shall never make thee shrink;
And Christ receive thy saule.

10

If meat or drink thou ne'er gavest nane,
Every night and all,
The fire shall burn thee to the bare bane;
And Christ receive thy saule.

[1] Bridge

II

This ae night, this ae night,
Every night and all,
Fire and selte and candle-light,
And Christ receive thy saule.

(14)

The Golden Vanitie

I

There was a ship called *The Golden Vanitie*,
And she feared to be taken by a Turkish gallee[1].
Sailing by the Lowlands.

2

Out spake the little ship-boy, out spake he:
'What if I shall sink you that Turkish gallee?'

3

Out spake the captain, and out spake he:
'Silver and gold I'll give you for a fee.'

4

'Then row[2] me up tight in a black bull's skin,
And throw me over deck-board, sink I or swim!'

5

They have rowed him up tight in a black bull's skin
And thrown him over deck-board, sink he or swim.

[1] galley: ship propelled by oars   [2] tie

36

6

About and about and about went he,
Until he came up with the Turkish gallee.

7

Some were playing cards, and some were at dice,
As with his auger sharp in her side he bored thrice.

8

Then with his auger sharp again he bored thrice:
Till the water rushed in and dazzled their eyes.

9

Some cut their cloaks, and some cut their caps,
To try if they might stop the salt water gaps.

10

About and about and about went he,
Until he came back to *The Golden Vanitie*.

11

'Now cast me a rope and pull me up on board,
And prove unto me as good as your word!'

12

'I will cast you no rope,' the captain he cried.
'Farewell, for now I leave you to drift with the tide.'

13

Then out spake the ship-boy, and out spake he:
'O, what if I sink you, as I sunk the gallee?'

14

Then when his messmates saw how he drifted with the tide,
They cast him a rope, but on deck-board he died.
      Sailing by the Lowlands.

Young Beichan

1

Young Beichan, he was a noble lord
  And a peer of high degree;
He hath taken ship at London Town,
  For that Christ's Tomb he would see.

2

He sailéd west, and he sailéd east
  Till he came to Galilee,
Where he was cast in prison strong
  And handled cruelly.

3

Now in that prison there grew a tree,
  Was wondrous tall and strong;
He was gyvéd[1] by the middle to 't,
  That his life might not be long.

4

The Turk he had a daughter fair,
  Ne'er fairer did man see,
She's stolen the keys of the prison house door,
  Young Beichan to set free.

5

'O, gin a lady would borrow[2] me,
  At her stirrup-foot I would run.
Or gin a widow would borrow me,
  I would swear to be her son.

---

[1] fettered   [2] redeem me

6

'Or gin a virgin would borrow me,
   I would wed her with a ring,
I'd give her halls, I'd give her bowers,
   I'd love her above all thing.'

7

O barefoot, barefoot gaed she but[1],
   And barefoot came she ben[2],
It was not for want of hosen and shoon,
   But for fear of making din.

8

And when she saw him, Young Beichán,
   Her heart was wondrous sair:
For the mice but and[3] the bold ratóns[4]
   Had eaten his yellow hair.

9

She gave him a shaver for his beard,
   A comber for his hair,
Five hundred pound in his pockét:
   To spend and not to spare.

10

'Go, set your foot on good shipboard,
   And haste to your ain countrie,
And before three years are come and gone
   Well married we shall be.'

11

He had not been in his ain countrie
   A twelvemonth till an end,
But he must marry an earl's daughtér,
   Or else lose all his land.

[1] to the outer room of a house   [2] to the inside room   [3] and also   [4] rats

12

'Ochone alas!' says Young Beichán,
   'I know not what to dee:
For I cannot win[1] to Burd[2] Isbel,
   And she cannot come to me.'

13

O, it fell once about that time,
   Burd Isbel lay asleep;
And up there starts the Billie Blin[3]
   That slept at her bed-feet.

14

'O waken, waken, Burd Isbél!
   How can ye sleep so sound,
When this is Beichan's wedding day,
   All upon English ground?

15

'Now do[4] ye to your mother's bower,
   Think neither sin nor shame,
But take ye two of your mother's maries[5]
   To keep ye from all blame.

16

'Then dress yourself in red scarlétt,
   And your maries in dainty green;
And put a girdle about your middle,
   Were fit for any queen.

17

'Then gang ye down by yon sea-side,
   And down by the sea-strand,
So bonny will the Holland boats
   Come rowing to your hand.

[1] reach   [2] lady   [3] a household demon   go   [5] ladies

18

'Then set your milk-white foot aboard
    And cry: "Hail ye, Domine!"
And I shall be the steerer o't
    To row you o'er the sea.'

*   *   *

19

She came full soon to Young Beichan's gate,
    And heard the fiddlers play;
Then well she kenned from all she heard
    It was his wedding day.

20

She's putten her hand in her pockét,
    And taken out guineas three.
'Hey, take ye that, ye proud portér,
    Bid the bridegroom speak to me!'

21

O, when that he came up the stair,
    He louted[1] to the knee:
'Won up[2], won up, ye proud portér,
    And what meaneth this courtesy?'

22

'O, I have been porter at these gates,
    It's thirty years and three;
But there's a lady at them now:
    Her like I ne'er did see.

[1] bowed   [2] rise up

23

'For she is dressed in red scarlétt,
　　Her maries dressed in green;
And she's a girdle about her middle
　　Were fit for any queen.

24

'On every finger she has a ring,
　　And on the mid-finger three;
And there's as much gold about her brow
　　Would buy an earldom for me.'

25

Then up it starts him, Young Beichán,
　　And he swears by Our Ladie:
'It can be none but Burd Isbel,
　　Come o'er the flood to me!'

26

O, quickly ran he down the stairs,
　　Of fifteen made but three;
He's taken Burd Isbel in his arms
　　And kissed her tenderly.

27

'O, have ye forgotten, Young Beichán,
　　The vow you made to me,
When I took you out of the prison strong
　　And helped you o'er the sea?

28

'O, have ye taken another bride,
　　And have ye forgotten me,
Though I stole the keys of the prison door,
　　And gave you liberty?'

29

She lookéd over her left shouldér
    To hide the tear in her ee:
'Now fare thee well, dear love,' she says,
    'And I'll think no more on thee.'

30

'Take home your daughter, madam,' he says,
    'With all my lands for fee;
For I must marry my first true love
    That gave me liberty.'

31

'Is this a custom of your house,
    Or the fashion of your town:
To marry a maid on a May morning
    And send her back ere noon?'

(16)

Johnny of Cockley's Well

1

Johnny he's risen up in the morn,
    Called for water to wash his han's;
But little knew he that his bloody hounds
    Were bound in iron banns,
    Were bound in iron banns.

2

Johnny's mother she's gotten word of that,
    And care-bed[1] she has ta'en:
'O, Johnny, for my benison,
    I beg you'll bide at hame;
For the wine so red, and the well-baken bread,
    My Johnny he shall want nane.

[1] almost sick-bed

3

'There are seven forsters[1] at Pickram Side,
   At Pickram where they dwell,
And for a drop of thy heartë's blood
   They would ride the fords of Hell.'

4

Johnny he's gotten word of that,
   And he's turned wondrous keen;
He's put him off the red scarlett,
   And he's put on the Lincoln green.

5

With a sheaf of arrows by his side,
   And a bent bow in his hand,
He's mounted on a prancing steed,
   And ridden fast o'er the land.

6

He's up in Braidhouplee, and down in Braidslee,
   And under a buss[2] of broom,
And there he found a good dun deer,
   Feeding in little room[3].

7

Johnny shot, and the dun deer leapt,
   And she leapt wondrous wide[4],
Until they came to the wan water,
   And he stemmed[5] her of her pride.

8

He's taken out the little pen-knife,
   'Twas full three quarters[6] long,
And he's taken out of that dun deer
   The liver but and the tongue.

[1] foresters   [2] bush   [3] space   [4] far   [5] ended
[6] three-quarters of a span, the span being the distance between the tip of the little finger and the top of the thumb when both are stretched out. The knife was 7 inches long, in fact

9

They ate of the flesh, and they drank of the blood,
  And the blood it was so sweet,
Which causéd Johnny and his bloody hounds
  To fall in a deep sleep.

10

By then came an old palmér,
  And an ill death may he die!
For he's away to Pickram Side,
  As fast as he can drie.[1]

11

'What news, what news?' says one of the forsters,
  'What news have ye brought to me?'
'I have no news,' the palmer said,
  'But what I saw with my ee.

12

'High up in Braidhouplee, low down in Braidslee,
  And under a buss of scroggs[2],
O there I spied a well-wight[3] man
  Sleeping among his dogs.

13

'His coat it was of the light Lincóln,
  And his breeches of the same,
His shoes were of the Cordovan leather,
  And gold buckles tying them.'

14

Up bespoke the seven forsters,
  Up bespoke they one and all:
'O, that is Johnny of Cockley's Well,
  And on him we shall fall.'

---

[1] manage   [2] stunted bushes   [3] bold, or sturdy

15

O, the first stroke that they gave him,
    They struck him by the knee;
Then up bespoke his sister's son:
    'O, the next'll gar[1] him dee!'

16

'O, some they count[2] ye well-wight men,
    But I do count ye nane;
For you might well have wakened me,
    And asked gin I would be ta'en[3].

17

'The wildest wolf in all this wood
    Would not have done so by me;
She'd have wet her foot in the wan watér,
    And sprinkled it o'er my brae[4],
And if that would not have wakened me,
    She'd have gone and let me be.

18

'O, bow of yew, if ye be true,
    In London, where ye were bought,
Fingers five, get up belive[5],
    Manhood shall fail me nought!'

19

Johnny he's killed the seven forstérs,
    He's killed them all but ane,
And that won scarce to Pickram Side,
    To carry the bode-words[6] hame.

[1] make
[4] brow

[2] value
[5] soon

[3] whether I would surrender
[6] fatal news

46

20

'Is there never a boy in all this wood
   That will tell what I can say:
That will go for me to Cockley's Well,
   Tell my mother to fetch me away?

21

'O, I often took to my mother's house
   The dun roe and the hare;
But today I'll send to my mother's house
   Much sorrow but and much care.'

22

There was a boy into that wood,
   That told what Johnny would say,
And many an ane was the well-wight man
   At the fetching of Johnny away.

(17)

The Unquiet Grave

1

O bonny, bonny sang the bird,
   Sat on the coil of hay[1],
But dowie, dowie[2] was the maid
   That loved the corpse of clay.

2

'Cold blows the wind on my true love,
   And a few small drops of rain;
I never had but one true love,
   And in greenwood he was slain.

---

[1] hay-cock   [2] doleful

3

'I'll do as much for my true love
    As any lover may;
I'll sit and mourn all on his grave
    A twelvemonth and a day.'

4

The twelvemonth and the day being gone,
    The ghost began to greet[1]:
'Your salten tears they trickle down,
    They wet my winding sheet.'

5

''Tis I, your love, sits on your grave
    And will not let you sleep;
For I crave one kiss of your clay-cold mouth,
    And that is all I seek.'

6

'O, lily, lily are my lips;
    My breath comes earthy strong;
If you have one kiss of my clay-cold mouth,
    Your time will not be long.'

7

'Is there any room at your head, Willíe?
    Is any room at your feet?
Is any room at your two sides,
    Wherein that I may creep?'

8

'There is no room at my head, Margrét,
    Nor any at my feet;
There is no room at my two sides,
    My coffin's made so meet[2].'

[1] cry   [2] narrow

9

''Tis down in yonder garden green,
　　Love, where we used to walk,
The finest flower that e'er was seen
　　Is withered to a stalk.'

10

'The stalk is withered dry, indeed,
　　So will our hearts decay;
O, make yourself content, my love,
　　Till Death calls you away.

11

'But plait a wand of bonny birk[1],
　　And lay it on my breast;
Then get you hame, my May Margrét,
　　And wish my soul good rest.'

(18)

Graeme and Bewick

1

Good Lord Graeme is to Carlisle gane,
　　Sir Robert Bewick there met he,
And arm in arm to the wine they did go,
　　And they drank till they were both merrie.

2

Good Lord Graeme, he has ta'en the cup:
　　'Sir Robert Bewick, and here's to thee!
And here's to our twa sons at hame
　　And billies[2] together aye may they be!'

[1] birch　　　　　　[2] companions-in-arms

3

'O, were your son a clerk like mine,
   And learned some books that he could read,
They might have been two brethren bold,
   And they might have bragged[1] the Border side.

4

'Aye, were your son a clerk like mine,
   Well learnéd in the grammarie[2]!
But your son's a lad, and he is but bad,
   And billy to my son he cannot be.'

5

Good Lord Graeme has a reckoning called,
   A reckoning full then called he;
And he paid a crown, and it went roun',
   It was all for the good wine and free.

6

And he has to the stable gane,
   Where there stood thirty steeds and three;
He's taken his ain horse among them all,
   And hame he rade sae hastily.

7

'Welcóme, my father!' said Christie Graeme,
   'But where sae long from hame were ye?'
'It's I have been at Carlisle town,
   And a baffled[3] man by thee I be.

8

'For I have been at Carlisle town,
   Where Sir Robert Bewick he met me;
He says ye're a lad, and ye are but bad,
   And billy to his son ye cannot be.

---

[1] defied   [2] book knowledge   [3] disgraced

'I sent ye to school, and ye would not learn;
  I bought ye books, and ye would not read;
Therefore my blessing ye shall never earn,
  Till I see with Bewick thou save my head[1].'

'Now, God forbid, my dear fathér,
  That ever such thing should be!
Billy Bewick was my master, and I was his scholar,
  And aye sae well as he learnéd[2] me.'

'O, hold thy tongue, thou limmer loon[3],
  And of thy talking let me be!
If thou doest not end me this quarrel soon,
  There is my glove, I'll fight wi' thee.'

Then Christie Graeme he stoopéd low
  Unto the ground, you shall understand.
'O father, put on your glove again
  The wind has blown it from your hand.'

'What's that thou sayest, thou limmer loon?
  How darest thou stand to speak to me?
If thou dost not end this quarrel soon,
  There's my right hand, thou shalt fight with me.'

Then Christie Graeme's to his chamber gane,
  To consider well what then should be;
Whether he should fight with his old fathér,
  Or with his billy Bewick, he.

---

[1] save my face   [2] taught   [3] rascally lout

'If I should kill my billy dear,
   God's blessing I shall never win;
But if I strike at my old fathér,
   I think 'twould be a mortal sin.

'And if I kill my billy dear,
   That is God's will, so let it be;
But I make a vow, ere I gang from hame,
   That I shall be the next man dee[1].'

Then he's put on his back a good old jack[2],
   And on his head a cap of steel,
And sword and buckler by his side;
   O, gin[3] he did not become them weel!

We'll leave off talking of Christie Graeme,
   And talk of him again belive[4];
And we will talk of bonny Bewick,
   Where he was teaching his scholars five.

When he had taught them well to fence,
   And handle swords without any doubt,
He took his ain sword under his arm,
   And he walked his father's close[5] about.

He looked between him and the sun,
   And all to espy what there might be,
Till he saw a man in armour bright,
   Was riding that way most hastily.

[1] to die   [2] coat of mail   [3] if   [4] soon   [5] garden

'O, who is yon, that comes this way,
   So hastily that hither came?
I think it be my brother dear,
   I think it be young Christie Graeme.

'Ye're welcome here, my billy dear,
   And thrice ye're welcome unto me!'
'But I'm woe to say, I've seen the day
   When I am come to fight with thee.

'My father's gane to Carlisle town,
   With your father Bewick there met he:
He says I'm a lad, and I am but bad,
   And a baffled man I trow I be.

'He sent me to school, and I would not learn;
   He bought me books, and I would not read;
So my father's blessing I'll never earn,
   Till he see how my arm can save his head[1].'

'O, God forbid, my billy dear,
   That ever such a thing should be!
We'll take three men on either side,
   And see if we can our fathers agree[2].'

'O, hold thy tongue now, billy Bewick,
   And of thy talking let me be!
But if thou'rt a man, as I'm sure thou art,
   Come o'er the dyke, and fight with me.'

[1] save his face   [2] make agree

'But I have no harness, billy, on my back,
  As well I see is now on thine.'
'But as little harness as is on thy back,
  As little, billy, shall be on mine.'

Then he's thrown off his coat of mail,
  His cap of steel away flung he;
He stuck his spear into the ground,
  And he tied his horse unto a tree.

Then Bewick has thrown off his cloak,
  And his psalter-book from his hand flung he;
He laid his hand upon the dyke,
  And over he leapt most manfully.

O, they have fought for twa lang hours;
  When twa lang hours were come and gane,
The sweat drapped fast from off them both,
  But a drop of blood could not be seen.

Till Graeme gave Bewick an awkward stroke,
  An awkward stroke strucken sickerly[1];
He has hit him under the left breast,
  And dead-woundéd to the ground fell he.

'Rise up, rise up now, billy dear,
  Arise and speak three words to me!
Whether thou hast gotten thy deadly wound,
  Or if God and good leeching may succour thee?'

[1] surely

33

'On horse, on horse now, billy Graeme,
   And get thee far from hence with speed;
And get thee out of this countrie,
   That none may know who has done the deed.'

34

'O, I have slain thee, billy Bewick,
   If this be true thou tellest to me;
But I made a vow, ere I came from hame,
   That aye the next man I would be.'

35

He has pitched[1] his sword in a moodie-hill[2],
   And he has leapt twenty lang feet and three,
And on his own sword's point he leapt,
   And dead upon the ground fell he.

36

'Twas then came up Sir Robert Bewick,
   And his brave son alive saw he;
'Rise up, rise up, my son,' he said,
   'For I think ye have gotten the victory.'

37

'O, hold your tongue, my father dear,
   Of your prideful talking let me be!
Ye might have drunken your wine in peace,
   And let your son and his billy be.

38

'Go, dig a grave, both wide and deep,
   And a grave to hold both him and me;
But lay Christie Graeme on the sunny side,
   For I'm sure he won the victory.'

---

[1] fixed   [2] mole-hill

39

'Alack! O, woe!' old Bewick cried,
  'Alack! was I not much to blame?
I'm sure I have lost the liveliest lad
  That e'er was born unto my name.'

40

'Alack! O, woe!' quoth good Lord Graeme,
  'I'm sure I have lost the deeper lack[1]!
I durst have ridden the Border through,
  Had Christie Graeme been at my back.

41

'Had I been led through Liddesdale,
  And thirty horsemen guarding me,
And Christie Graeme been at my back,
  So soon would he have set me free!

42

'I've lost my hopes, I've lost my joy,
  I've lost the key but and the lock;
I durst have ridden the world around,
  Had Christie Graeme been at my back.'

(19)

The Wife of Usher's Well

I

There lived a wife[2] at Usher's Well,
  And a wealthy wife was she;
She had three stout and stalwart sons
  And sent them over the sea.

---

[1] loss   [2] woman

They had not been a week from her,
   A week but barely ane,
When word came to the carlin wife[1]
   That her three sons were gane.

3

They had not been a week from her,
   A week but barely three,
When word came to the carlin wife
   That her sons she'd never see.

4

'I wish the wind may never cease,
   Nor fashes[2] in the flood,
Till my three sons come hame to me,
   In earthly flesh and blood.'

5

It fell about the Martinmas,
   When nights are long and mirk[3],
The carlin wife's three sons came hame,
   And their hats were of the birk[4].

6

It neither grew in dyke nor ditch,
   Nor yet in any sheugh[5];
But at the gates of Paradise,
   That birk grew fair eneugh.

★   ★   ★

7

'Blow up the fire, my maidens two,
   Bring water from the well;
For all my house shall feast this night,
   Since my three sons are well.'

[1] old woman   [2] troubles   [3] dark   [4] birch   [5] ditch, or furrow

8

And she has made to them a bed,
   She's made it large and wide,
And she's ta'en her mantle her about,
   Sat down at the bedside.

     ★   ★   ★

9

O, up then crew the red, red cock,
   And up and crew the grey;
The eldest to the youngest said:
   ''Tis time we were away.'

10

The cocks they had not crawed but once,
   And dinged[1] their breasts for day,
When the youngest to the eldest said:
   'Brother, we must away!

11

'The cock doth craw, the day doth daw[2]:
   The channerin'[3] worm doth chide;
Gin we be missed out of our place,
   A sair pain we must bide[4].

12

'Fare ye well, my mother dear,
   Farewell to barn and byre!
And fare ye well, the bonny lass
   That kindles my mother's fire!'

[1] struck   [2] dawn   [3] petulant   [4] expect

(20)

The Heron

The hern[1] flew east, the hern flew west,
She bare her over the fair forést.
Lully, lullay; lully, lullay;
The falcon hath stol'n my mate away.

2

She bare her up, she bare her down,
She bare her over the heath so brown.

3

She bare her over the meadows green.
And all to espy what might be seen.

4

O, then she saw an orchard fair,
Where groweth many an apple and pear.

5

And in that orchard there standeth a hall
That hangéd was with purple and pall.

6

And in that hall there standeth a bower
Was all clad over with lily flower.

[1] heron

7

And in that bower there standeth a bed
With silken sheets, and gold so red.

8

And in that bed there lieth a knight
Whose wounds are bleeding both day and night.

9

And under that bed there runneth a flood,
Was half of water and half of blood.

10

And by that bed there standeth a stone,
And a leal maidén was set thereon.

11

With silver needle and silken thread
Stemming[1] the wounds where they did bleed.
Lully, lullay; lully, lullay;
The falcon hath stol'n my mate away.

(21)

Johnny Faa, the Lord of Little Egypt

1

The gipsies came to lord Cassilis' gate,
And sang in the garden shadie.
They sang so sweet and so complete
That well they pleased his ladie.

[1] stopping

2

She has cast by her needle and thread,
    Let fall the embroidered linen;
For her heart it melted away like snow,
    To hear the gipsies singing.

3

O, then she came tripping down the stair
    With her two maids before her,
And when they saw her well-faur'd[1] face
    They cast their glamour[2] o'er her.

4

She gave to them the good wheat bread,
    And she gave to them the ginger;
But to Johnny she gave a far better thing—
    The gold ring from her finger.

5

'Will you come with me, my honey, my heart,
    Will you come along, my dearie?
For I will vow by the hilt of my sword
    Your lord shall no more come near ye.'

6

'Maids, take from me my silk manteel
    And bring unto me a plaidie:
For I will travel the wide world o'er
    Along with this gipsie laddie.'

7

She has pluckéd off her high-heeled shoon,
    Were made of Spanish leather,
And she's gone barefoot with black Johnny Faa
    Among the rocks and heather.

[1] handsome   [2] magic

8

'I could walk the hills with my Johnny Faa,
　And never would I be wearie;
I could sail the seas with my Johnny Faa,
　To sink or swim with my dearie.'

9

They wandered high, they wandered low,
　They wandered late and earlie,
Until they came to a crofter's[1] barn
　And wow, but she was wearie!

10

'Last night I climbed to a goose-feather bed,
　Where my good lord climbed before me;
But now I must lie on the bracken leaf,
　With a black crow glowering o'er me.'

11

'O, hold your tongue, my honey, my heart,
　O, hold your tongue, my dearie,
For I do vow by the moon and the stars
　Your lord shall no more come near ye.'

12

They wandered near, they wandered far,
　They wandered both together;
Until they came to the wan water,
　Was grown about with heather.

13

'Now bend your back, my honey, my heart,
　Now bend it down, my bonnie,
And carry me over this wan water
　It's you shall be my pownie[2].'

[1] small farmer　　　[2] pony

14

'I have often rode through that wan watér,
  And my noble lord beside me;
But now with my white feet I must wade
  And carry this gipsie laddie.'

15

Lord Cassilis, he came home at e'en,
  And he speired[1] of the maids for his ladie;
The one she cried, the other replied:
  'She's away with a gipsie laddie.'

16

'Go, saddle me my black, black horse,
  The brown rides not so speedie;
Before that ever I eat or drink
  I shall bring me home my ladie!'

17

O, he rode high and he rode low,
  The black, black horse ran speedie;
Until he came to the wan watér
  And there he espied his ladie.

18

'Last night we lay in a goose-feather bed,
  So snug we lay together;
Why wentst thou off with a gipsie gang
  Among these rocks and heather?

19

'Wilt thou not come home, my honey, my heart,
  Wilt thou not come home, my dearie?
For I'll close thee fast in a private room,
  Where no man may come near thee.'

[1] asked

'Nay, I'll go not home, my lord,' she said,
  'And I'll not be thy dearie;
I have brewed good beer, I'll drink of the same,
  And thou shalt come not near me.

'Yet will I swear by the moon and the stars,
  And the bright sun shining o'er me,
That I am as free of the gipsie gang
  As the hour my mother bore me!'

*   *   *

They were fifteen valiant gipsie men,
  That were black, but very bonnie.
And were all put down for one light wife[1]:
  The Earl of Cassilis' honey.

(22)

King John and the Abbot

I

An ancient story I'll tell you anon,
Of a notable prince, that was called King John;
In England was born, and showed great might,
Though he did much wrong and maintained little right.
  Derry down, down hey, derry down.

[1] unfaithful woman

Now this is a story, a story, so merry,
Concerning the Abbot of Canterbury,
It was for his housekeeping, and his good cheer,
He came into danger, as you shall hear.

3

'How now, Father Abbot? I've heard the cry[1]
That thou keepest a far better house than I;
And for thy housekeeping and high renown,
I fear thou has treason against my crown.

4

'A hundred men, as I have heard say,
Thou keepest about thee every day;
And fifty gold chains without any doubt,
In velvet coats do wait thee about.'

5

'My liege, in my city it well is known
That I spent no money but what's my own.'
'Nay, if thou dost not answer me questions three,
Thy head shall be taken from thy bodie.

6

'First: when I am set so high on my steed
With my crown of gold put upon my head,
Amongst all my nobles, with joy and much mirth
Thou must tell to one penny what I am worth.

7

'And this second question thou shalt not flout:
How soon I may ride the whole world about.
And from the third question thou must not shrink
But tell me truly what I do think.'

[1] report

8

'O, these are hard questions for my poor wit,
And I cannot answer them all as yet;
But if you will give me twenty days' space,
I'll do my endeavour to please Your Grace.'

9

'O, twenty days full I will thee give,
For that is the longest thou hast to live.
And if thou dost not answer these questions right,
Thy head shall part from thy body that night.'

10

The abbot he thought on his liege's word,
And rode between Cambridge and Oxenford;
But never a doctor he found so wise
Could shew him these questions to enterprise[1].

11

Therewith the old abbot was nothing glad,
But he in his heart grew heavy and sad,
And hied him into his own countrie
To ease some part of his melancholy.

12

A shepherd was going back to his fold,
When he spied the abbot come over the wold[2].
'How now, Master Abbot? You're welcome home;
What news have you brought from good King John?'

13

'Sad news, sad news I have thee to give:
I have now but a week's space longer to live;
If I do not answer him questions three,
My head will be parted from my bodie.

---

[1] how to undertake   [2] downs

14

'When he is set so high on his steed,
With his crown of gold put upon his head,
Amongst his nobles, with joy and much mirth,
I must tell to one penny what he is worth.

15

'And (saith he) the next question I shall not flout:
How soon he may ride the whole world about.
And from the third question I must not shrink:
But tell him truly what he doth think.'

16

'O, Master, hast never heard it yet,
That a fool may learn[1] a wise man wit?
Lend me but your horse and your apparel,
I'll ride unto London and settle the quarrel.'

17

The shepherd he rode to the Court anon,
And the abbot's apparel he now had on,
That as soon as the King the shepherd did see,
He cried: 'Father Abbot, thou'rt welcome to me!

18

'And now I am set so high on my steed,
With my crown of gold put upon my head,
Amongst all my nobles, with joy and much mirth,
Thou must tell to one penny what I am worth.'

19

'For thirty pence was our dear Lord sold,
Unto the false priests, as we have been told,
And I think it will give Your Grace no offence
That I rate you at nine-and-twenty pence.'

[1] teach

20

The King he laughed, and swore by Saint Bittel[1]:
'I did not know I was worth so little.
And now the next question thou may'st not flout:
How soon may I ride the whole world about?'

21

'Thou must rise with the sun, and keep with the same,
Until the next morning he rises again.
For then Your Grace can have never a doubt
But in twenty-four hours you'll ride it about.'

22

The King he laughed, and swore by Saint Bride[2]:
'I did not know how fast I might ride.
Now from the third question thou shalt not shrink,
But tell me truly what I do think.'

23

'Ay, that I can do, and 'twill make you merry;
For you think I'm the Abbot of Canterbury.
Though I'm but his poor shepherd, as you may see,
Come here to beg pardon for him and for me.'

24

The King he laughed, and swore by his head:
'Thou shalt be the Abbot in t'other's stead!'
'Nay, nay, Your Grace, there is no such need,
For I ken neither to write nor to read.'

25

'Why, then,' quoth the King, 'I'll give thee clear
A patent of three hundred pounds a year.
And tell the old Abbot, when thou comest home,
Thou hast brought him a pardon from good King John.'

[1] St. Botolph   [2] St. Bridget

Get Up and Bar the Door

I

There lived a man at the foot of a hill,
    John Blunt it was his name;
And he sold liquor and yill[1] of the best,
    Which earned him wondrous fame.

2

Now it fell about the Martinmas time
    (And a gay time it was than[2]),
That Janet his wife did puddings make
    And boiled them in the pan.

3

The wind blew cold from north to south,
    It blew across the floor;
Quoth old John Blunt to Janet his wife:
    'Rise up and bar the door!'

4

'My hands are in my housewife keep[3],
    Good man, as ye may see,
And if ye will not bar it yerself
    It will ne'er be barred by me.'

5

They made a paction[4] 'twixt them twain,
    They made it firm and sure,
That the one that spake the foremost[5] word
    Was to rise and bar the door.

[1] ale   [2] then   [3] housewifely tasks   [4] compact   [5] first

6

Then by there came two gentlemen,
  Were riding over the moor;
And they came unto John Blunt's house
  Just by the light of the door.

7

'Now whether is this a rich man's house,
  Or whether is it a poor?'
But never a word spake man or wife
  For the barring of the door.

8

They came within and bade them good e'en,
  And syne bade them good morrow;
But never a word spake man or wife,
  For the barring of the door, O.

9

O, first they ate the white puddíng,
  And syne they ate the black;
Though Janet thought muckle[1] to herself,
  Yet never a word she spake.

10

O, syne they drank of the liquor so strong,
  And syne they drank of the yill.
'O, now we have gotten a house of our own
  I'm sure we may take our fill.'

11

Then said one gentleman to his friend:
  'Here, man, take thou my knife,
Do thou scrape off this goodman's beard
  While I kiss his goodwife.'

[1] much

'But there's no water in the house—
   How shall I shave him than?'
'What ails thee[1] with the pudding bree[2]
   That boils within the pan?'

O, up then started old John Blunt,
   And an angry man was he:
'Will ye kiss my wife before mine eyes
   And scald me with pudding-bree?'

Then up then started Janet his wife,
   Gave three skips upon the floor:
'Goodman, ye've spoken the foremost word,
   Get up and bar the door!'

(24)

Loving Mad Tom

From the hag[3] and hungry goblin
   That into rags would rend ye,
The spirits that stand by the naked man
   In the Book of Moons[4] defend ye,
That of your five sound senses
   You never be forsaken
Nor wander from yourselves, with Tom,
   Abroad to beg your bacon.

[1] what's wrong
[2] brew—the water in which the puddings had been cooked
[3] Black Annis, a goddess of the Old Religion who devoured children
[4] an astrological treatise by the 'Moon-men' or gipsies

While I do sing 'Any food, any feeding,
   Feeding, drink or clothing?
Come, dame or maid, be not afraid:
   Poor Tom will injure nothing.'

2

Of thirty bare years have I
   Twice twenty been enragéd[1],
And of forty been three times fifteen
   In durance soundly cagéd,
On the lordly lofts of Bedlam
   With stubble soft and dainty,
Brave bracelets strong, sweet whips ding-dong,
   And wholesome hunger plenty.
And now I sing, etc.

3

A thought I took for Maudline
   In a cruse of cockle pottage[2]:
With a thing thus tall—sky bless us all!—
   I befell into this dotage.
I've slept not since the Conquest,
   Ere then I never wakéd
Till the roguish fay of love where I lay
   Me found and stripped me naked.
And now I sing, etc.

4

When I short have shorn my sow's-face
   And snigged my hairy barrel[3],
At an oaken inn I pound[4] my skin
   In a suit of gilt apparel.

---

[1] insane   [2] cockle soup   [3] trimmed the hair on my belly
[4] impound

The Moon's my constant mistress,
   And the lovely owl my marrow[1].
The flaming drake[2] and the night-crow make
   Me music to my sorrow.
While I do sing, etc.

5

The palsy plague my pulses
   If I prig[3] your pigs or pullen[4],
Your culvers[5] take, or matchless[6] make
   Your Chanty-clear[7] or Solan[8]!
When I want provant[9], with Humphrey
   I sup, and when benighted
I repose in Paul's with walking saules
   Yet never am affrighted.
But I do sing, etc.

6

I know more than Apollo,
   For oft when he lies sleeping
I see the stars at bloody wars
   And the wounded welkin weeping,
The Moon embrace her shepherd[10]
   And the Queen of Love her warrior,
When the first doth horn[11] the Star of the Morn
   And the next, the Heavenly Farrier.
While I do sing, etc.

7

The gipsies, Snap and Pedro,
   Are none of Tom's comradoes;
The punk[12] I scorn and the cut-purse sworn
   And the roaring-boy's[13] bravadoes:

[1] dear companion   [2] dragon   [3] steal   [4] poultry   [5] doves   [6] widowed
[7] cock   [8] gander   [9] need food   [10] Endymion   [11] is unfaithful to
[12] low woman   [13] armed bully

73

The meek, the white, the gentle
   Me handle, touch and spare not,
But those that cross Tom Rhinoceros
   Do what the panther dare not.
Though I do sing, etc.

8

With an host of furious fancies
   Whereof I am commander,
With a burning spear and a horse of air
   To the wilderness I wander.
By a knight of ghosts and shadows
   I summoned am to tourney,
Ten leagues beyond the wide world's end—
   Methinks it is no journey.
Yet will I sing, etc.

9

I'll bark against the Dog Star,
   I'll crow away the morning,
I'll chase the Moon till it be noon
   And make her leave her horning,
But I'll find merry mad Maudline,
   And seek whate'er betides her,
And I will love beneath or above
   The dirty earth that hides her
Till then I sing, etc.

The Dead Brother

1

'How came that blood on thy coat-lap?
  O dear love, tell me.'
'It is the blood of my gay goshawk[1],
  That flew so fair and free.'
'It doth look too red for thy gay goshawk,
  That flew so fair and free.

2

'How came that blood on thy coat-lap?
  O dear love, tell me.'
'It is the blood of my good greyhound
  That traced the fox for me.'
'It doth look too red for the good greyhound
  That traced the fox for thee.

3

'How came that blood on thy coat-lap?
  O dear love, tell me.'
'It is the blood of my good roan mare
  That well would run for me.'
'It doth look too red for the good roan mare
  That well would run for thee.

4

'How came that blood on thy coat-lap?
  O dear love, tell me.'
'It is the blood of my dear brothér,
  The truth I'll tell to thee.'

[1] large, short-winged hawk

5

'And what did you fall out about?
  O dear love, tell me.'
'About some little bit of bush
  That soon would have made a tree.'

6

'And what wilt thou do now, my love?
  O dear love, tell me.'
'I'll set my foot in a naked[1] ship
  And sail across the sea.'

7

'And when wilt thou come home again?
  O dear love, tell me.'
'When the sun shines bright from the northern airt[2],
  And that shall never be.'

(26)

Chevy Chase

1

Earl Percie of Northumberland
  A vow to God did make:
His pleasure in the Scottish woods
  Three summer's days to take,

2

The fattest harts in Chevy Chase
  To kill and bear away.
The child may rue that is unborn
  The hunting of that day.

---

[1] without mast, sails or oars—the traditional punishment for parricide
[2] quarter of the sky

3

Earl Percie out of Bamborough came
 And brought a great meanie,[1]
With fifteen hundred archers bold,
 Were chosen from shires three.

4

These tidings to Earl Douglas came
 In Scotland where he lay.
'By my faith,' the doughty Douglas cried,
 'I will let[2] him if I may!'

5

It began upon a Monnynday,
 Ere daylight did appear;
The drivers through the woodës went
 To raise the fallow deer.

6

The bowmen cleft them to the hearts
 As down the brae they came;
And greyhounds through the greves[3] did rin:
 To them it was good game.

7

O, long before the sun was high
 An hundred harts were slain.
But when they had both dined and drunk
 They went to it again.

8

Lord Percie bade them blow a mort[4],
 And went to view the deer;
Quoth he: 'Earl Douglas promise made
 This day to meet me here.

[1] army   [2] prevent   [3] groves
[4] hunting call which announces the death of the quarry

9

'And if I thought he would not come,
  No longer would I bide.'
It's then a squire of Northumberlánd
  Looked out at the far braeside.

10

'Lo, yonder doth Earl Douglas come,
  With him a great meanie!
Hardier men of heart or hand
  Are not in Christiantie.

11

'Twenty hundred spearmen good,
  I reckon without fail
Were borne along on the flood of Tweed,
  From the bounds of Tividale.

12

'Leave off the bryttling[1] of the deer,
  And to your bows take heed,
For never yet since ye first them drew
  Have ye stood in so great need!'

13

The doughty Douglas on a steed
  Rode all his men beforn[2];
His armour glittered as it were gold:
  No bolder man was born.

14

'Tell me whose men ye are,' he said,
  'Or what man may he be
That bade you hunt in Chevy Chase
  In the spite of mine and me?'

---

[1] carving up   [2] in front of

The first that did him answer make
 It was the Earl Percie:
'We list not to declare nor show,
 My lord, what men we be;
But we will hunt here in the chase
 In the spite of thine and thee!

'Myself did swear a solemn oath
 In Bamborough, where I lay,
The fattest harts of Chevy Chase
 To kill and bear away.'

'I know thee well, an earl thou art,
 Lord Percie, so am I.
And for this hunting of Chevy Chase
 One of us twain shall die!

'Yet, by my faith, it were pitie
 These bowmen good to kill:
For they are guiltless of offence,
 'Tis ye have done me ill.

'Let thou and I this battle try,
 And set our men aside.'
'Christ's curse on his crown,' said Earl Percie,
 'By whom this be denied!'

Then spake the squire of Northumberland,
 Witherington was his name:
'It shall never be told in South Englánd
 To King Harrie the Fourth, for shame,

21

'That I saw my captain fight a fight
   And looking on did stand;
Nay, while I may yet my weapon wield
   I will help both heart and hand!'

22

The English archers bent their bows,
   Their aim it was full true;
At the first flight of flos[1] they sent
   Full fourscore Scots they slew.

23

The Douglas parted his host in three
   Like a chieftain great of pride;
With sure spears cut of mighty tree
   They come in on every side.

24

But ever again our good bowmén
   Gave many a wound full wide;
Many a doughty man they slew,
   Which gainéd them great pride.

25

Then did they let their bowës be,
   And pulled out brands full bright.
It was a heavy sight to see
   Such swords on basnets[2] light[3].

26

And greater grief it was to see
   How each man chose his spear,
And how the blood out of their breasts
   Did gush like water clear.

[1] arrows   [2] helmets   [3] fall

27

The Douglas and the Percie met,
    Like captains of might and main;
They swapped[1] together until they swot[2]
    With swords of fine Milaine[3],
And the red blood from their basnets sprent[4]
    As it were a shower of rain.

28

'O, yield thee, Percie,' the Douglas cried.
    'In faith I shall thee bring
Where thou shalt have an earlë's wage
    Of Jamie, our Scottish King.

29

'And thou shalt have thy ransom free,
    I swear you now this thing:
For the manfullest man thou art indeed
    That I met in field fighting.'

30

'Nay, Douglas,' quoth the lord Percie,
    'For I told it thee beforn:
That I would never yield in fight
    To no man of woman born.'

31

With that, there came an arrow keen,
    Sped of an English bow;
It strike Earl Douglas on the breast
    A deep and deadly blow.

[1] exchanged blows   [2] sweated   [3] steel made at Milan
[4] spurted

Through liver and through lungës both
   The keen arrów is gone,
That never after in his life-days
   He spoke more words than one,
Was: 'Fight ye, my merry men, whilst ye may
   For my life-days be done!'

Earl Percie leanéd on his sword
   And saw the Douglas dee;
He took the dead man by the hand
   And said: 'I'm woe for thee!

'To save thy life I would have left
   My lands for years full three;
No better man, of heart nor hand,
   Was in all the North Countrie.'

Then up there came a Scottish knight,
   Was Sir Hugh Montgomerie.
He saw the Douglas piercéd through
   And he took his mighty tree
For to ride upon his corsiare[1]
   Through an hundred archerie.

He set upon the Earl Percie
   A dint that was full sair,
With a sure thrust of his mighty tree
   Clean through his body he bare.

[1] courser

At t'other side a man might see
    A large clothyard or mair;
Two better captains did never live
    Than fell in battle there.

38

An archer of Northumberland
    Saw slain the Earl Percie;
An arrow of a clothyard long
    Unto his ear haled[1] he.

39

Against Sir Hugh Montgomerie
    His shaft full right[2] he set,
The grey goose wing that was thereon
    In his heart's blood was wet.

40

There was never a freck[3] one foot would flee,
    But steadfast all did stand,
Hewing at each other while they might
    With many a baneful brand.

41

This battle began in Cheviot
    An hour before the noon,
And when the evensong bell was rung
    The battle was not half done.

42

They went their way on either side
    By the light of stars and moon:
Many had no strength for to stand
    The Cheviot Hills aboon[4].

[1] pulled   [2] straight   [3] bold man   [4] above

43

Of fifteen hundred archers of England
    Went away but seventy-three,
Of twenty hundred spearmen of Scotland,
    Fifty-five, but hardily[1].

44

There was slain with the Earl Percie
    Sir John of Egerton,
Sir Roger, the lord of Hartly he was,
    And Sir William the bold Herón.

45

Sir George, the worthy Lumelley,
    A knight of great renown,
Sir Ralph the Rich of Ruggebie,
    With dints were beaten down.

46

For Witherington my heart was woe
    That ever he slain should be,
For when one leg was stricken off
    He fought upon t'other knee.

47

And with Earl Douglas there was slain
    Sir Hugh Montgomerie,
Sir Davie Laudale that with him rode,
    (His sister's son was he).

48

Sir Charles à Murray, from that place
    Who never a foot would flee,
Sir Hugh Maxwéll, that was a lord
    But savéd could not be.

[1] hardly

So, on the morrow they made them biers,
   Of birk and hazel grey,
Many widóws with weeping tears
   Did fetch their mates away.

Word is comen to Edinbro',
   To Jamie, the Scottish King;
It was of the death of Earl Douglás,
   His hands then he did wring

For the Lord Lieutenant of his Marchés,
   And cried: 'O, woe is me!
Such another captain my land within
   In faith shall never be.'

Word is comen to lovely London,
   To Harrie the Fourth, our King.
It was of the death of Earl Percie;
   His hands he too did wring.

'Now, God be with him,' said King Harrie,
   'Sith[1] it will no better be,
But I trust I have within my realm
   Five hundred as good as he.

since

'Yet shall not my cousin Jamie brag
    That I did not vengeance take,
To be revenged upon them all
    For brave Earl Percie's sake.'

This vow the King did well perform
    After, on Humbledown,
Where six and thirty Scottish knights
    In a day were beaten down.

At Otterburn began this fight,
    Upon a Monnynday[1],
There was the doughty Douglas slain,
    And the Percie went not away.

There was ne'er a time on the Marchparties[2]
    Since the Douglas and Percie met,
But it was marvail if the blood ran not
    As the rain doth run in the street.

Then Jesus Christ our balës[3] beat[4],
    And to the Bliss us bring;
Thus was the hunting of Cheviot,
    God send us good endíng!

[1] Monday   [2] Borderland   [3] troubles   [4] abate

Waly, Waly

1

O waly, waly[1], up the bank!
  And waly, waly, down the brae!
And waly, waly, yon burnside,
    Where I and she were wont to gae!

2

I leaned my back unto an aik,
  I thought it was a trusty tree;
But first it bowed, and syne it brake,
    Sae my true love did lightly[2] me.

3

O waly, waly! but love be bonny
  A little time, while it is new;
But when 'tis old, it waxeth cold,
    And fades away like morning dew.

4

O, wherefore should I busk[3] my head?
  Or wherefore should I kaim my hair?
For my true love has me forsook,
    And says he'll never love me mair.

[1] alas, alas!   [2] treat me lightly   [3] adorn

5

Now Arthur-Seat[1] shall be my bed,
    The sheets shall ne'er be fyled[2] by me;
Saint Anton's well shall be my drink,
    Since my true love's forsaken me.

6

Martinmas wind, when wilt thou blow,
    And shake the green leaves off the tree?
O, gentle death, when wilt thou come?
    For of my life I am wearie.

7

'Tis not the frost that freezes fell[3],
    Nor blowing snow's inclemency—
'Tis not such cold that makes me cry,
    But my love's heart grown cold to me.

8

When we came in by Glasgow Town,
    We were a comely sight to see:
My love was clad in black velvét,
    And I myself in cramasie[4].

9

But had I wist, before I kissed,
    That love had been so ill to win,
I'd have locked my heart in a case of gold,
    And pinned it with a silver pin.

[1] by Edinburgh   [2] soiled   [3] evilly   [4] crimson

O, O, if my young babe were born,
    And set upon the nurse's knee,
And I myself were dead and gone!
    For a maid again I'll never be.

(28)

Barbara Allan

1

It was about the Martinmas time,
    When thick the leaves were falling,
That Sir John Graeme of the West Countrie,
    Sent word for Barbara Allan.

2

His men have gone through Scarlet Town,
    To the place where she was dwelling,
With: 'Haste and come to my master dear,
    Gin ye be Barbara Allan!

3

'There's sorrow printed on his face,
    And death is o'er him stealing.
And he is sick, and very sick,
    For love of Barbara Allan.'

4

'If sorrow's printed on his face
    And death is o'er him stealing,
Then little better shall he be
    For a sight of Barbara Allan.'

5

So hooly, hooly[1] raise she up,
   And came where he was lying.
She drew the curtain by, and said:
   'Young man, I think you're dying.'

6

'O, it's I am sick, and very sick,
   And it's all for Barbara Allan.'
'O, the better for her ye ne'er shall be,
   Though your heart's blood were spilling.

7

'Do not you mind, young man,' said she,
   'How, with the townsfolk melling[2],
Ye made the healths go round and round
   And slighted Barbara Allan?

8

'Gin now on your sickbed you lie,
   And death with you be dealing;
Why should I pity on you take?
   Farewell!' said Barbara Allan.

9

He turned his face unto the wall,
   Since she of hope had reft him,
Then hooly, hooly, raise she up
   And to his sorrow left him.

[1] slowly   [2] mixing

10

She had not gone of miles but two
　　When she heard the dead bell ringing,
And every jow[1] the dead bell gave
　　Cried: 'Woe to Barbara Allan!'

11

'O, mother, mother, make my bed,
　　O, make it soft and narrow,
Since my love died for me today,
　　I'll die for him tomorrow.'

(29)

Robin Hood and the Three Squires

1

There are thirteen months in all the year,
　　As I hear many men say.
But the merriest month in all the year
　　Is the merry month of May.

2

Now Robin Hood is to Nottingham gone,
　　With a link-a-down and a-day,
And there he met a silly[2] old woman,
　　Was weeping on the way[3].

3

'What news? What news, thou silly old woman?
　　What news, I do thee pray?'
Said she: 'Three squires in Nottingham town
　　Are condemned to die this day.'

---

[1] stroke　　　[2] simple　　　[3] road

4

'O, have they parishes burned?' he said,
  'Or have they ministers slain?
Or have they robbéd any virgín,
  Or other men's wives have ta'en?'

5

'They have no parishes burned, good sir,
  Nor yet have ministers slain,
Nor have they robbed any virgín,
  Nor other men's wives have ta'en.'

6

'O what have they done?' said bold Robin Hood,
  'I pray thee tell to me.'
'It's for slaying of the King's fallow deer,
  Bearing their bows with thee.'

7

'Dost thou not mind[1], old woman,' he said,
  'How thou madest me sup and dine?
By the truth of my body,' quoth bold Robin Hood,
  'You'd not tell this in better time!'

8

Now Robin Hood is to Nottingham gone,
  With a link-a-down and a-day,
And there he met with a silly old palmer[2],
  Was walking along the highway.

[1] remember   [2] a pilgrim from the Holy Land

9

'What news? What news, thou silly old man?
  What news, I do thee pray?'
Said he: 'Three squires in Nottingham Town
  Are condemned to die this day.'

10

'Come, change thy apparel with me, old man,
  Come, change thy apparel for mine!
Here is forty shillings in good silvér,
  Go, drink it in beer or wine.'

11

'O, thine apparel is good,' he said,
  'And mine is ragged and torn;
Wherever you go, wherever you ride,
  Ne'er laugh an old man to scorn.'

12

'Come, change thy apparel with me, old churl[1].
  Come, change thy apparel with mine!
Here are twenty pieces of good broad gold,
  Go, feast thy brethren with wine.'

13

Then he put on the old man's hat,
  It stood full high on the crown:
'The first bold bargain that I come at,
  It shall make thee come down.'

[1] countryman

14

Then he put on the old man's cloak,
   Was patched black, blue and red;
He thought it no shame all the day long
   To wear the bags of bread.

15

Then he put on the old man's breeks,
   Were patched from side to side.
'By the truth of my body,' bold Robin 'gan say,
   'This man loved little pride.'

16

Then he put on the old man's hose,
   Was patched from knee to wrist.
'By the truth of my body,' said bold Robin Hood,
   'I'd laugh if I had any list[1].'

17

Then he put on the old man's shoes,
   Were patched both beneath and aboon.
Then Robin Hood swore a solemn oath:
   'It's good habit[2] that makes a man.'

18

Now Robin Hood is to Nottingham gone,
   With a link-a-down and a-down,
And there he met with the proud sheriff,
   Was walking along the town.

[1] wish   [2] clothes

19

'O save, O save, O sheriff,' he said,
   'O save, and you may see!
And what will you give to a silly old man
   Will today your hangman be?'

20

'Some suits, some suits,' the sheriff he said,
   'Some suits I'll give to thee;
Some suits, some suits, and pence thirteen
   Today is a hangman's fee.'

21

Then Robin he turns him round about,
   And jumps from stock[1] to stone;
'By the truth of my body,' the sheriff he said,
   'That's well jumped, thou nimble old man!'

22

'I was ne'er a hangman in all my life,
   Nor yet intend to trade;
But curst be he,' said bold Robin,
   'That was first a hangman made.

23

'I've a bag for meal, and a bag for malt,
   And a bag for barley and corn;
A bag for bread, and a bag for beef,
   And a bag for my little horn.

[1] stump

24

'I have a horn in my pockét,
  I got it from Robin Hood,
And still when I set it to my mouth,
  For thee it blows little good.'

25

'O wind[1] thy horn, thou proud fellów,
  Of thee I have no doubt;
I wish that thou give so loud a blast
  Till both thy eyes fell out.'

26

The first loud blast that Robin did blow,
  He blew both loud and shrill;
A hundred and fifty of Robin Hood's men
  Came running over the hill.

27

The next loud blast that he did give,
  He blew both loud and amain,
And a hundred more of Robin Hood's men
  Came running over the plain.

28

'O, who are yon,' the sheriff he said,
  'Come tripping over the lea?'
'They're my attendants,' brave Robin did say,
  'They'll pay a visit to thee.'

[1] put wind into

They took the gallows from the slack[1],
They set it down in the glen,
They hanged the proud sheriff on that,
And they freed their own bold men.

(30)

The Holy Land of Walsinghame

1

'As ye came from the holy land
Of Walsinghame,
Met you not with my true love
By the way as ye came?'

2

'How should I know your true love,
That have met many a one
As I came from the holy land,
That have come, that have gone?'

3

'She is neither white nor brown,
But as the heavens fair;
There is none hath her divine form
In the earth, in the air.'

[1] pass between two hills

4

'Such a one did I meet, good sir,
    Such an angelic face,
Who like a nymph, like a queen, did appear
    In her gait, in her grace.'

5

'She hath left me here alone
    All alone, as unknown,
Who sometime did me lead with herself,
    And me loved as her own.'

6

'What's the cause that she leaves you alone
    And a new way doth take,
That sometime did you love as her own,
    And her joy did you make?'

7

'I have loved her all my youth,
    But now am old, as you see:
Love likes not the falling fruit,
    Nor the withered tree.'

8

'Know that love is a careless child,
    And forgets promise past:
He is blind, he is deaf when he list,
    And in faith never fast.

9

'His desire is a dureless[1] content,
   And a trustless joy;
He is won with a world of despair,
   And is lost with a toy.

10

'Of womenkind such indeed is the love,
   (Or the word love abused),
Under which many childish desires
   And conceits are excuséd.

11

'But true love is a durable fire,
   In the mind ever burning,
Never sick, never dead, never cold,
   From itself never turning.'

(31)

Sir Andrew Barton

1

As it befell in midsummertime,
   When birds sing sweetly on every tree,
Our noble king, King Henry the Eighth,
   Over the river of Thames passed he.

[1] not lasting

He was no sooner over the river,
  Down in a forest to take the air,
But eighty merchants of London City
  Came kneeling before King Henry there.

3

'O, ye are welcome, rich merchánts,
  Good sailors, welcome unto me!'
They swore by the rood they were sailors good,
  But rich merchánts they could not be.

4

'To France nor Flanders dare we not pass,
  Nor a Bordeaux voyage we cannot fare,
And all for a riever[1], Andrew Barton,
  That robs us of our merchants' ware.'

5

King Henry was stout, and he turned him about,
  And swore by the Lord that was mickle of might,
'I thought there lived no man in this world
  That durst have wrought England such unright[2].'

6

But ever they sighed, with 'Woe betide',
  And unto King Henry they answered again:
'He is a proud Scot that will rob us all
  Were we twenty ships and he but ane.'

[1] robber   [2] wrong

7

The King looked over his left shoulder,
  Amongst his lords and barons so free:
'Have I never a man in all my land
  Will fetch yon traitor unto me?'

8

'Yes, that dare I!' saith Charles, my lord Howard,
  Near to the King whereas he did stand;
'If that Your Grace will give me the place,
  Myself will be the only man.'

9

'Thou shalt have six hundred men,' saith King Henry,
  'And choose them out of my realm so free;
Besides both mariners and boys,
  To guide your great ship on the sea.'

10

'I'll go speak with Sir Andrew,' saith Charles, my lord Howard,
  'Upon the sea, if he be there;
I will bring him and his ship to shore,
  Or before my prince I will never come near.'

11

The first of all my lord called then
  A noble gunner he was ane;
This man was three score years and ten,
  And Peter Simon was his name.

12

'Peter,' saith he, 'I must sail the sea,
  To seek out an enemy; God be my speed!
Before all others I have chosen thee
  Of an hundred gunners to be the head.'

13

'My lord,' saith he, 'if you've chosen me
 Of an hundred gunners to be the head,
Hang me at your main-mast tree
 If I miss my mark past twelvepence bread[1].'

14

The next of all my lord he did call,
 A noble bowman he was ane;
In Yorkshire was this gentleman born,
 And William Horsley was his name.

15

'Horsley,' saith he, 'I must sail the sea,
 To seek out an enemy; God be my speed!
Before all others I have chosen thee
 Of an hundred bowmen to be the head.'

16

'My lord,' saith he, 'if you've chosen me
 Of an hundred bowmen to be the head,
Hang me at your main-mast tree
 If I miss my mark past threepence bread.'

17

With pikes, and guns, and shot and bowmen,
 This noble Howard is gone to sea,
On the day before midsummer even,
 And out at Thames mouth sailéd he.

[1] breadth

18

Three days forth they had not sailéd
   Upon their journey they took in hand,
But there they met with a noble ship,
   And stoutly made it both stay and stand.

19

'Thou must tell me thy name,' saith Charles, my lord Howard,
   'And I'll bind thee with an oath so strong,
Come, tell me where thy dwelling is,
   And to what port thy ship doth belong.'

20

'My name is Henry Hunt, my lord Howard,
   With a pure heart and a penitent mind;
I and my ship they do belong
   Unto the Newcastle that stands upon Tyne.'

21

'Now, thou must tell me, Harry Hunt,
   As thou hast sailéd by day and by night,
Didst thou not hear of a stout robbér?
   Men call him Sir Andrew Barton, Knight.'

22

But ever he sighed, and said: 'Alas!
   Full well, my lord, I know that wight;
Full well I know him to my misaunter[1],
   For I was his prisoner but yesternight.

[1] misfortune

23

'As I was sailing upon the sea,
    And a Bordeaux voyage as I did fare,
To his hatch-board, he claspéd me,
    And robbéd me of my merchants' ware.

24

'Now I am a man both poor and bare,
    And all will have their own of me,
Therefore to London I shall fare,
    To make complaint to my prince Henrie.'

25

'O, that shalt not need,' saith my lord Howard,
    'If thou canst let me this robber see,
For every penny he took thee fro,
    A shilling,' he said, 'shall be thy fee!'

26

Saith Henry Hunt: 'Now God forfend,
    My lord, you should work so far amiss!
God keep you out of that traitor's hand!
    For you little ken what a man he is.

27

'He is brass within, and steel without,
    And beams he bears in his top-castle strong;
His ship hath ordnance clean round about;
    And of fighting Scots he commands a throng.

'He hath a pinnace, is dearly dight[1],
   Saint Andrew's cross, that is his guide[2];
And it bears nine score good men and more,
   Besides fifteen cannons on every side.

'Had you twenty cannons, and he but ane,
   Either on hatch-board[3] or in haul[4],
He would o'ercome you with might and main,
   If but his beams he let down fall.'

'This is cold comfort,' saith my lord Howard,
   'To welcome a stranger thus to sea;
Yet I'll bring both him and his ship to shore,
   Or else to Scotland he shall bring me.'

'Then get thee a noble gunner, my lord,
   That can well a gun set with his ee,
For to sink his pinnace by the board,
   And, after, o'ercome he may be.

'And when that you have done him so,
   If you chance Sir Andrew for to board,
Let no man to his top-castle go—
   And I will give you a glass[5], my lord,

[1] richly adorned   [2] flag   [3] deck   [4] hold   [5] spy-glass

33

'And then you shall need to fear no Scot,
  Whether you sail by day or night,
For tomorrow morn, by se'en of the clock
  You shall meet with Sir Andrew Barton, Knight.

34

'I was his prisoner but yesternight,
  And he hath taken me sworn[1],' quoth he;
'I trust my Lord God will me forgive
  An if that oath then broken be.

35

'Lend me six pieces, and lend me shot,
  Into my ship to sail the sea,
And I swear tomorrow, by nine of the clock,
  Your honour again then will I see.'

*   *   *

36

Now the hatch-board where Sir Andrew lay
  Was hatched with gold so dearly dight:
'O, by my faith,' Lord Howard did say,
  'But yonder Scot is a worthy wight!

37

'Take in your ancients[2], take in your standards,
  Yea, that no man shall them see,
And put me forth a white willow wand,
  Such as merchants use to sail the sea.'

[1] put me on parole not to reveal his whereabouts   [2] ensigns

38

But they stirred neither top nor mast[1],
 Whenas Sir Andrew they passéd by:
'What English are yonder,' saith Sir Andrew,
 'That ken so little courtesy?

39

'Of the seas I have been admirál,
 I have ruled them for years more than three,
And no English dog nor Portingall
 Has come this way without leave of me.

40

'But now yon pedlars, they are gone past,
 Which is no little grief to me:
Go, fetch them back!' saith Sir Andrew Barton.
 'I will hang them from my main-mast tree.'

41

With that the pinnace drew out full fast,
 That my lord Howard might it well ken;
Its shot struck down my lord's foremast,
 And killed fourteen of my lord his men.

42

'Come hither, Simon!' saith my lord Howard,
 'Look that thy words be true thou said;
For I'll hang thee at my main-mast tree
 If thou miss thy mark past twelvepence bread.'

[1] they did not dip in greeting

Simon was old, but his heart was bold;
   He took a piece and laid it full low:
He put in chain shot nine yards long,
   Besides other great shot less and mo'.

With that he let his great gun blaw[1];
   So well he settled it with his ee:
The first sight that Sir Andrew saw,
   Was his pinnace sinking in the sea.

O, when he saw what the shot had done,
   Lord! in his heart he was not well:
'Cut my ropes! 'Tis time to be gone!
   For I'll fetch yon pedlars back mysel'!'

When my lord Howard then saw him loose,
   Lord! in his heart but he was fain[2]:
'Strike on your drums! Spread out your ancients!
   Sound out your trumpets! Sound them amain!'

'Fight on, my men!' saith Sir Andrew Barton;
   'Wot[3], howsoever this fight shall sway,
It is my lord Admirál of England
   Hath come to see me on the sea.'

---

[1] blow off   [2] glad   [3] know

Simon had a son, with a shot of a gun—
 And well Sir Andrew might it ken—
For he shot it in at a privy place,
 And killed sixty more of Sir Andrew's men.

Harry Hunt came in at the other side,
 And at Sir Andrew he shot then;
He felled the fore-mast that was his pride,
 And killed eighty more of Sir Andrew's men.

'I have done a good turn unto this knight,
 For I wot he was never our King's friend;
He had near undone me yesternight,
 But I think I have quit him well in the end.'

'Ever alas!' saith Sir Andrew Barton,
 'What should a man either think or say?
Yonder false thief is my strongest foe,
 Who was my prisoner but yesterday.

'Come hither to me, thou good Gordóun,
 And be thou ready at my call,
And I will give thee three hundred poun'
 If thou will let my beams down fall.'

53

With that he swarved[1] the main-mast tree,
 So did he it with might and main;
Horsley, with a bearing[2] arrow,
 Stroke the Gordoun through the brain.

54

With that he fell to the hatches again,
 Sore of the wound then did he bleed;
'Covetousness gets no gain,
 It is very true,' as the Welshman said.

55

'Come hither to me, James Hamiltóun,
 My sister's son I can thee call;
I'll give to thee six hundred poun'
 If thou will let my beams down fall.'

56

With that he swarved the main-mast tree,
 So did he it with might and main:
Horsley, with another arrow,
 Strake the yeoman through the brain.

57

That he fell down to the hatches again;
 Sore of his wound then he did bleed;
And word went through Sir Andrew's men
 That the yeoman he was dead.

[1] swarmed up [2] death-bearing

But when he saw his sister's son slain,
　Lord! in his heart he was not well:
And Sir Andrew then his oath hath ta'en:
　'I will let fall yon beams mysel'!

'Go fetch me here my armour of proof,
　The which is gilded with gold so clear;
God be with my brother, John of Barton!
　Against the Portingalls he did it wear.'

But when he got his armour of proof,
　And when his body he put it on,
Then every man that thought thereof,
　Said: 'Gun nor arrow he need fear none.'

'Come hither, Horsley!' saith my Lord Howard,
　'And look thy shaft that it go right;
Shoot a good shot in the time of need,
　And for this thou shalt be made a knight.'

'I'll do my best,' said Horsley then,
　'Your honour shall see before I go;
If I should be hanged at your main-mast tree,
　I have at my side but arrows two.'

63

Then Horsley spied a privy place,
   Beneath the spole[1] of his right knee;
And he let fly his bearing arrow
   And pinned him to the main-mast tree,

64

That Sir Andrew therefrom could not win free,
   Though he sought to swarve with might and main;
Over the collar then of his jack
   He struck Sir Andrew through the brain.

65

'Fight on, my men!' saith Sir Andrew Barton,
   'Though I be hurt, I am not slain;
I'll lay me down and bleed awhile,
   But then I'll rise and fight again.

66

'Fight on, my men!' saith Sir Andrew Barton,
   'These English dogs they bite so low;
Fight on for Scotland and Saint Andrew,
   Until you hear my whistle blow!'

67

But when they could not hear his whistle,
   Saith Harry Hunt: 'I'll lay my head,
You may board yon noble ship, my lord,
   For I trow Sir Andrew he is dead.'

[1] knee-joint

68

With that they boarded the noble ship,
　So did they it with might and main;
They found eighteen score Scots were quick[1],
　Besides the rest were maimed or slain.

69

My lord Howard hath taken a sword in hand,
　And hath cut off Sir Andrew's head;
The Scots, they did round about him stand,
　But never a word they spoke for dread.

70

He hath gared the body be taken down,
　And over the hatch-board cast in sea,
With about his middle three hundred poun':
　'Wherever thou land'st, it will bury thee.'

71

Into England with his head they voyaged,
　With right good will, and force, and main;
And on the day before New Year's E'en,
　Into Thames mouth they came again.

72

My lord Howard rode to King Henry's place,
　With all the news that he could him bring:
'Such a New Year's gift I have brought your Grace
　As never did subject to any king.

73

'For merchandize and for manhóod,
    The like to them was never found;
The sight thereof would do you good,
    There was never the like on English ground.'

74

And when the King heard it was my lord Howard,
    Full royally then he welcomed him hame.
Sir Andrew's ship was his New Year's gift,
    And braver ship you never saw nane.

75

Now hath our King Sir Andrew's ship,
    Beset with pearls and precious stane[1];
Now hath our England two ships of war,
    Two ships of war, before but ane.

76

'Who holp to this?' saith good King Henry,
    'That I may reward him for his pain.'
'Harry Hunt, and Peter Simon,
    William Horsley, and I the same[2].'

77

'Harry Hunt shall have his whistle and chain,
    And all his jewels, whate'er they be,
And other rich gifts that I'll not name,
    For the good service he hath done me.

[1] stone   [2] myself

78

'Thou shalt be a knight, good William Horsley,
  Lands and livings thou shalt have store.
Howard shall be Earl of Nottingham,
  And so was never Howard before.

79

'Now, Peter Simon, thou art old;
  I will maintain thee and thy son;
Thou shalt have five hundred pound in gold
  For the good service that thou hast done.'

80

Then King Henry shifted his room;
  In came the Queen and her ladies bright;
Other errands they had none
  But to see Sir Andrew Barton, Knight.

81

But when they saw his deadly face,
  With the eyes hollow in his head:
'I would give a hundred pound,' quoth his Grace,
  'That he were alive as he is dead!

82

'Yet for the manful part he did play,
  When he was sailing upon the sea,
His men shall have half a crown a day
  Till they come to my brother, King Jamie.'

(32)

Bruton Town

1

In Bruton Town there lived a farmer,
  That had two sons and one daughter dear.
By day and night they were contriving
  To fill their parents' hearts with fear.

2

One told his secret to none other,
  But unto his brother this he said:
'I think our servant courts our sister,
  I fear they have a mind to wed.'

3

'If he our servant courts our sister,
  That maid from such a shame I'll save:
I'll put an end to all their courtship,
  I'll send him silent to his grave.'

4

A day of hunting was prepared,
  In thorny woods, where briars grew:
There they did then that young man murder
  And in the brook his body threw.

5

'Now welcome home, my dear young brothers!
  Our serving man, is he behind?'
'We left him where we have been hunting,
  We left him where no man may find.'

6

To bed she went then, crying and lamenting,
  Lamenting for her heart's delight.
She slept, she dreamed, she saw him by her
  All bloody-red in piteous plight.

7

His lovely curls were wet with water,
  His body all agape with blows.
'O love, for thee I suffer murder,
  For thee I lie where no man knows.'

8

She rose up early the morrow morning,
  Unto the forest brake she rode,
And there she found her own dear jewel
  All dabbled o'er in a gore of blood.

9

Dabbled o'er both with blood and water,
  And thus she did her true love find,
She drew a kerchief from her pocket
  And wiped his eyes, though they were blind.

The Death of Robin Hood

I

Robin dwelt in greenë wood
   Full twenty year and two,
And to the court of Edward our King
   Again he would not go.

2

But it befell upon a time
   That Robin, who was so hale,
His broad arróws they fled not right[1]
   And his strength began to fail.

3

'I will never drink strong ale,' said Robin,
   'Nor meat will do me good,
Until I have gone to Kirkeslie Hall
   My veinës for to let blood.'

4

'That I rede[2] not,' said Will Scathelock.
   'By the assent of me,
Unless three score of thy best bowmén
   Do follow thither with thee.

[1] straight   [2] counsel

'For the dame priór, thy aunt's daughtér,
  Of merry Kirkeslie Hall,
She hath fallen in love with a gallant knight,
  Red Roger do men him call.

'Now this Sir Roger of Doncaster
  Will be sure to flyte[1] with thee;
But if thou hast need of us bowmen,
  In faith we will not flee.'

'Thou hast said thy say, now, William Scathelock,
  At home I rede thou be.'
'If you be wroth, my dear mastér,
  Thou'lt hear no more of me.'

Said Robin: 'No man shall with me go,
  Nor no man with me ride,
Save that Little John, whom well I love,
  Shall bear a bow by my side.'

'I'll bear thy bow,' saith Little John,
  'If thou'lt shoot a penny with me.'
To that bold Robin did make assent,
  And cried: 'John, so let it be!'

[1] quarrel

These two bold archers have shotten together
 At a penny shot they rank[1];
And then they came to a black watér
 And over it lay a plank.

Upon the plank knelt an old widów,
 Was banning of Robin Hood.
'Why doest thou this?' saith Little John,
 'For he is my master good.'

'I had a tall son,' the widow said,
 'And he was the Sheriff's man.
But Robin him slew with a broad arrów,
 And therefore I him ban.'

Then Little John drew out his sword,
 The old widow for to kill.
'That I rede not,' saith Robin Hood,
 'Such vengeance would be but ill.'

Then they went on, and farther on,
 And nothing more did see,
Until they came to a bank of broom,
 Where maidens there wept three.

[1] boldly

15

'Why weep ye, maidens?' saith Little John,
   'Why make ye all this moan?'
'There hath come a word that Robin Hood
   To Kirkeslie Hall is gone.

16

'We have a tear, and many a tear,
   To give for Robin Hood,
We weepen for his dear bodie
   That today must be let blood.'

17

'Nay, the dame priór is my aunt's daughtér,
   Thus are we nigh of kin.
I know she would harm me not this day
   The whole world for to win.'

18

But ever they sighed, and said 'alas',
   And let the tears down fall
With: 'Beware, Sir Roger of Doncaster
   Is her own speciál[1]!'

19

Forth then went those archers two
   And never did they lin[2],
Until they came to Kirkeslie Hall
   And tirled upon a pin[3];
Up then there rose the dame priór,
   And let good Robin in.

[1] particular lover   [2] stop   [3] knocked at the door

20

'Sit down, sit down, good cousin!' she said,
　'And drink some beer with me!'
'Nay, I will neither eat nor drink
　Until thou'st blooded me.

21

'And for that service thou'lt do for me,
　Here is twenty pound in gold.'
With that he drew it from his purse;
　Let her have more if she wold[1].

22

'Well, I have a room, good cousin,' she said,
　'Which thou didst never see.
And if thou please to walk therein
　Well blooded shalt thou be.'

23

She took him with her lily white hand,
　And to the room him led.
'Go, shoot awhile in yonder forest,
　Good Little John,' he said.

24

'Now bide thou here,' saith the dame priór,
　'Good cousin, by the fire.
And I will fetch my blood-irons now
　And give thee thy desire.'

[1] wanted

25

Then into the room she came again,
  She came again in that ilk[1]:
With a pair of blood-irons in her hands,
  Were rowéd all in silk.

26

'Set a chafing dish to the fire,' she said,
  'And strip thou up thy sleeve.'
(I hold him but an unwise man
  That will no warning leeve[2].)

27

She laid the blood-irons to his vein,
  And from it shrank not he.
She pierced the vein and pierced it well,
  Alack, it was pitie!

28

And syne came out the thick, thick blood,
  And syne came out the thin,
And well then wist him Robin Hood
  Treason was there within.

29

For into the chamber came Red Roger,
  That like a ghost did glide,
And where Robin sat, with a grounden glave[3]
  Did pierce his milk-white side.

[1] in this following style   [2] believe   [3] sharpened sword

Though Robin was weak and heavy of foot,
    Yet he bated[1] Roger's pride,
For with his sword between shoulder and head
    He dealt a wound full wide.

'Lie there, lie there, Red Roger,' he saith,
    'Thou'lt be the dogs' repast!'
But the dame priór, that watched behind,
    Did lock the door full fast.

Then Robin might not get him thence,
    Though to break the door he tried,
And forth of the strait shot-windów[2]
    I trow he could not glide.

He bethought him then of his bugle horn,
    That hung down low to his knee;
He set the horn unto his mouth
    And blew him faint blasts three.

Then Little John the faint blasts heard,
    As he leaned against a tree.
'I fear my master is near to death,
    He blows so wearilie.'

[1] put an end to   [2] narrow window through which to shoot arrows

35

Then Little John to the Hall is gone,
  As fast as he can dree[1];
And when he came to the private room
  The door he brake in three.

36

There he saw Robin by the fire,
  And Red Roger lying dead,
And the chafing-dish was overflowed,
  And the floor with blood ran red.

37

'A boon, a boon!' saith Little John,
  And he fell upon his knee.
'It is to burn down Kirkeslie Hall,
  And all this nunnerie.'

38

'Now nay: now nay,' quoth Robin Hood,
  'That boon I'll not grant thee,
For I never hurt woman in all my life,
  Nor at mine end shall it be.

39

'But give me my bent bow in my hand,
  And a broad flo I'll let flee,
And where the same shall be taken up
  My grave shall diggéd be.

[1] manage

40

'Lay me this bright sword at my head,
   These arrows at my feet;
And lay this yew-bow by my side
   That made me music sweet.

41

'Let me have length and breadth enough,
   With a green sod under my head,
That they may say, that pass my grave:
   "Here Robin Hood lieth dead!" '

42

He's done him to the shot-window,
   And wondrous far he shot;
Though the flo it sped four hundred yards,
   Little John he missed it not[1].

43

Then Robin he yielded up the ghost,
   That no word more spake he.
But Little John his grave hath digged—
   It was hard by Kirkeslie.

(34)

The Gaberlunzie Man

I

The pawky auld carle[2] came o'er the lea,
Wi' many good e'ens and days to me,
Saying: 'Goodwife, for your courtesie,
   Will you lodge a silly poor man?'

[1] did not fail to recover it   [2] humorous old fellow

The night was cauld, the carle was wat;
And down ayont the ingle[1] he sat;
My daughter's shoulders he 'gan to clap,
    And cadgily[2] ranted and sang.

2

'O wow!' quo' he, 'were I as free
As first when I saw this countrie,
How blythe and merry wad I be!
    And I wad never think lang.'
He grew canty[3], and she grew fain,
But little did her auld minny ken
What thir slee twa[4] thegither were say'ng,
    When wooing they were sae thrang.

3

'And O,' quo' he, 'an ye were as black
As e'er the crown of my daddy's hat,
'Tis I wad lay thee by my back,
    And awa' wi' me thou shou'd gang.'
'And O,' quo' she, 'an I were as white
As e'er the snaw lay on the dike,
I'd cleed me braw[5] and ladylike,
    And awa' wi' thee I wad gang.'

4

Between the twa was made a plot
They rose a wee before the cock,
And wilily they shot the lock,
    And fast to the bent[6] are they gane.

[1] in the chimney corner   [2] cheerfully   [3] affectionate
[4] sly two   [5] I'd clad me brave   [6] tall grass

Up in the morn the auld wife rase,
And at her leisure put on her claise;
Syne to the servant's bed she gaes,
　　To speer[1] for the silly poor man.

5

She gaed to the bed where the beggar lay;
The strae[2] was cauld, he was away,
She clapt her hands, cry'd: 'Waladay,
　　For some of our gear will be gane!'
Some ran to coffer and some to kist[3],
But nought was stown[4] that cou'd be mist;
She danc'd her lane[5], cry'd: 'Praise be blest,
　　I have lodg'd a leal poor man!

6

'Since naething's awa', as we can learn,
The kirn's to kirn[6], and the milk to earn,
Gae but the house, lass, and waken my bairn,
　　And bid her come quickly ben[7].'
The servant ga'ed where the daughter lay,
The sheets were cauld, she was away,
And fast to her goodwife did say:
　　'She's aff with the gaberlunzie[8] man.'

7

'O fy gar ride, and fy gar rin,
And haste ye find these traitors again;
For she's be burnt and he's be slain,
　　The wearifu' gaberlunzie man.'

[1] inquire　　　　　[2] straw　　　[3] chest　　　[4] stolen　　　[5] by herself
　　[6] the handmill must be turned　　　　　　[7] to the inner room
　　　　　　　　　[8] professional beggar

Some rade upo' horse, some ran a-fit[1],
The wife was mad, and out o' her wit,
She cou'd na gang, nor yet cou'd she sit,
    But she curs'd ay, and she bann'd.

8

Meantime far 'hind out o'er the lea,
Fu' snug in a glen, where nane cou'd see,
The twa, with kindly sport and glee,
    Cut fro a new cheese a whang[2]:
The priving[3] was good, it pleas'd them baith,
To lo'e her for ay, he gae her his aith.
Quo' she: 'To leave thee I will be laith,
    My winsome gaberlunzie man.

9

'O kenned my minny I were wi' you,
Ill-faurdly wad she crook her mou'[4];
Sic a poor man she'd never trew[5],
    After the gaberlunzie man.'
'My dear,' quo' he, 'ye're yet o'er young,
And hae na learn'd the beggars' tongue,
To follow me frae town to town,
    And carry the gaberlunzie on.'

10

'Wi' cauk and keel[6] I'll win your bread,
And spindles and whorles for them wha need,
Whilk is a gentle trade indeed,
    To carry the gaberlunzie on.

¹ on foot   ² slice   ³ provant, food
⁴ She would give her mouth an ugly twist   ⁵ trust
⁶ chalk and ruddle: i.e. he'll draw a customer's likeness in white and red

I'll bow my leg, and crook my knee,
And draw a black clout o'er my e'e;
A cripple or blind they will ca' me,
    While we shall be merry and sing.'

(35)

Admiral Benbow

1

Come, all ye seamen bold
    And draw near, and draw near,
Come, listen to my song
    And have no fear:
'Tis of an Admiral's fame,
And John Benbow was his name—
How unto his end he came
    You shall hear, you shall hear.

2

John Benbow he set sail
    For to fight, for to fight.
Until Du Casse's ships
    They hove in sight.
He after them made sail
With a fine and pleasant gale,
But his captains they turned tail,
    In affright, in affright.

3

Said Kirby unto Wade:
    'Let us run! Let us run!'
To Kirby, Wade replied:
    'Ay, let's have done,

For I value no disgrace
Nor the losing of my place
But I swear I will not face
    Shot of gun, shot of gun!'

4

So brave Benbow sailed alone
    On that day, on that day.
Alone against the French,
    Where they lay;
He fought them with a frown,
Till the blood came trickling down—
And he earned a great renown
    On that day, on that day.

5

Brave Benbow lost his leg
    By chain shot, by chain shot;
Yet all the pain he bore
    He valued not;
Brave Benbow lost his leg
But his company he did beg:
'Fight on, lads, don't reneg[1]!
    'Tis our lot, 'tis our lot!'

6

A surgeon dressed his wound;
    Cried Benbow, cried Benbow:
'Nay, to my cabin, faith,
    I will not go!
Let a cradle[2] now in haste
On the quarter-deck be placed!'
And with fury still he faced
    England's foe, England's foe.

[1] break your oath of loyalty   [2] a support for his shattered leg

Wednesbury Cocking

1

At Wednesbury there was a cocking,
  A match between Newton and Scroggins;
The colliers and nailers left work,
  And all to old Spittle's went jogging.
To see this noble sport,
  Many noblemen resorted;
And though they'd but little money,
  Yet that little they freely sported.

2

There was Jeffery and Colborn from Hampton,
  And Dusty from Bilston was there;
Plummery he came from Darlaston,
  And he was as rude as a bear.
There was old Will from Walsall,
  And Smacker from Westbromwich come;
Blind Robin he came from Rowley,
  And staggering he went home.

3

Ralph Moody came hobbling along,
  As though he some cripple were mocking,
To join in the blackguard throng,
  That met at Wednesbury cocking.

He borrowed a trifle of Doll,
    To back old Taverner's grey;
He laid fourpence-halfpenny to fourpence,
    He lost and went broken away.

4

But soon he returned to the pit,
    For he'd borrowed a trifle more money,
And ventured another large bet,
    Along with blubbermouth Coney.
When Coney demanded his money,
    As is common on all such occasions,
He cried: 'Rot thee, if thee don't hold thy rattle,
    I'll pay thee as Paul paid the Ephesians.'

5

Scroggins' breeches were made of nankeen,
    And worn very thin in the groin,
When he stooped to handle his cock,
    His buttocks burst out behind!
Besides, his shirt tail was beshet,
    Which caused among them much laughter,
Scroggins turned around in a pet[1],
    And cried: 'Damn ye all, what's the matter?'

6

The morning's sport being over,
    Old Spittle a dinner proclaimed,
Each man he should dine for a groat[2],
    If he grumbled he ought to be maimed.

[1] fury   [2] cheaply

For there was plenty of beef,
    But Spittle he swore by his troth
That never a man should dine
    Till he'd ate his noggin of broth.

7

The beef it was old and tough,
    Of a bull that was baited to death,
Barney Hyde got a lump in his throat,
    That had like to have stopped his breath;
The company all fell in confusion,
    At seeing poor Barney Hyde choke,
So they took him into the kitchen,
    And held him over the smoke.

8

They held him so close to the fire,
    He frizzled just like a beefsteak,
They then threw him down on the floor,
    Which had like to have broken his neck.
One gave him a kick in the stomach,
    Another a clout on the brow,
His wife said: 'Throw him into the stable,
    And he'll be better just now.'

9

Then they all returned to the pit,
    And the fighting went forward again;
Six battles were fought on each side,
    And the next was to décide the main.
For these were two famous cocks
    As ever this country bred,
Scroggins' a duck-winged black,
    And Newton's a shift-winged[1] red.

[1] of two colours

The conflict was hard on both sides,
    Till Brassy's shift-winged was choked;
The colliers were tarnationly vexed,
    And the nailers were sorely provoked.
Peter Stevens he swore a great oath
    That Scroggins had played his cock foul;
Scroggins gave him a kick on the head,
    And cried: 'Yea, God damn thy soul!'

The company then fell in discord,
    A bold, bold fight did ensue;
Kick, bludgeon and bite was the word,
    Till the Walsall men all were subdued.
Ralph Moody bit off a man's nose,
    And wished that he could have him slain,
So they trampled both cocks to death,
    And they made a draw of the main.

The cock-pit was near to the church,
    An ornament unto the town;
On one side an old coal pit,
    The other well gorsed around.
Peter Hadley peeped through the gorse,
    In order to see the cocks fight;
Spittle jobbed out his eye with a fork,
    And said: 'Rot thee, it served thee right!'

Some people may think this strange,
    Who Wednesbury Town never knew;
But those who have ever been there,
    Won't have the least doubt it is true;

For they are so savage by nature,
    And guilty of deeds the most shocking;
Jack Baker he whacked his own father,
    And thus ended Wednesbury Cocking.

(37)

The Children in the Wood

1

Now ponder well, you parents dear,
    These words which I shall write;
A doleful story you shall hear,
    In time brought forth to light.
A gentleman of good account
    In Norfolk dwelt of late,
Who did in honour far surmount
    Most men of his estate.

2

Sore sick he was and like to die,
    No help his life could save;
His wife by him as sick did lie,
    And both possessed one grave.
No love between these two was lost,
    Each was to other kind;
In love they lived, in love they died,
    And left two babes behind:

3

The one a fine and pretty boy
    Not passing three years old,
The other a girl more young than he,
    And framed in beauty's mould.

The father left his little son,
    As plainly did appear,
When he to perfect age should come,
    Three hundred pounds a year;

4

And to his little daughter Jane
    Five hundred pounds in gold,
To be paid down on marriage-day,
    Which might not be controlled.
But if the children chanced to die
    Ere they to age should come,
Their uncle should possess their wealth;
    For so the will did run.

5

'Now, brother,' said the dying man,
    'Look to my children dear;
Be good unto my boy and girl,
    No friends else have they here:
To God and you I recommend
    My children dear this day;
But little while be sure we have
    Within this world to stay.

6

'You must be father and mother both,
    And uncle, all in one;
God knows what will become of them
    When I am dead and gone.'

With that bespake their mother dear:
  'O, brother kind,' quoth she,
'You are the man must bring our babes
  To wealth or misery!

7

'And if you keep them carefully,
  Then God will you reward;
But if you otherwise should deal,
  God will your deeds regard.'
With lips as cold as any stone,
  They kissed their children small:
'God bless you both, my children dear!'
  With that the tears did fall.

8

These speeches then their brother spake
  To this sick couple there:
'The keeping of your little ones,
  Sweet sister, do not fear;
God never prosper me nor mine,
  Nor aught else that I have,
If I do wrong your children dear
  When you are laid in grave!'

9

The parents being dead and gone,
  The children home he takes,
And brings them straight unto his house,
  Where much of them he makes.

He had not kept these pretty babes
  A twelvemonth and a day,
But, for their wealth, he did devise
  To make them both away.

10

He bargained with two ruffians strong,
  Which were of furious mood,
That they should take these children young,
  And slay them in a wood.
He told his wife an artful tale:
  He would the children send
To be brought up in London Town
  With one that was his friend.

11

Away then went those pretty babes,
  Rejoicing at that tide,
Rejoicing with a merry mind
  They should on cock-horse ride.
They prate and prattle pleasantly,
  As they ride on the way,
To those that should their butchers be
  And work their lives' decay:

12

So that the pretty speech they had
  Made Murder's heart relent;
And they that undertook the deed
  Full sore did now repent.
Yet one of them, more hard of heart,
  Did vow to do his charge,
Because the wretch that hired him
  Had paid him very large.

13

The other won't agree thereto,
    So here they fall to strife;
With one another they did fight
    About the children's life:
And he that was of mildest mood
    Did slay the other there,
Within an unfrequented wood—
    The babes did quake for fear!

14

He took the children by the hand,
    Tears standing in their eye,
And bade them straightway follow him,
    And look they did not cry;
And two long miles he led them on,
    While they for food complain:
'Stay here,' quoth he. 'I'll bring you bread
    When I come back again.'

15

These pretty babes, with hand in hand,
    Went wandering up and down;
But never more could see the man
    Approaching from the town.
Their pretty lips with blackberries
    Were all besmeared and dyed;
And when they saw the darksome night,
    They sat them down and cried.

16

Thus wandered these poor innocents,
    Till death did end their grief;
In one another's arms they died,
    As wanting due relief:

No burial this pretty pair
  From any man receives,
Till Robin Redbreast piously
  Did cover them with leaves.

17

And now the heavy wrath of God
  Upon their uncle fell;
Yea, fearful fiends did haunt his house,
  His conscience felt an hell:
His barns were fired, his goods consumed,
  His lands were barren made,
His cattle died within the field,
  And nothing with him stayed.

18

And in a voyage to Portugal
  Two of his sons did die;
And to conclude, himself was brought
  To want and misery:
He pawned and mortgaged all his land
  Ere seven years came about.
And now at last his wicked act
  Did by this means come out.

19

The fellow that did take in hand
  These children for to kill,
Was for a robbery judged to die,
  Such was God's blessèd will:
Who did confess the very truth,
  As here hath been displayed:
The uncle having died in jail,
  Where he for debt was laid.

20

You that executors be made,
  And overseërs eke,
Of children that be fatherless,
  And infants mild and meek,
Take your example by this thing,
  And yield to each his right,
Lest God with suchlike misery
  Your wicked minds requite.

(38)

The Banished Duke of Grantham

1

Three youths went a-fishing
  Down by yon seaside,
And they saw a dead body
  Cast up by the tide.

2

This youth said to that youth,
  These words I heard him say:
"Tis the banished Duke of Grantham,
  And the tide's on its way!'

3

They took him up to Portsmouth,
  To the place where he was known,
And from thence up to London,
  The place where he came from.

4

They drew out his bowels,
  They stretchéd out his feet,
And they balméd his body
  With spices fresh and sweet.

5

They set him in his coffin,
  They raised him from the ground,
Nine lords followed after.
  While the trumpets did sound.

6

O, black was their mourning,
  And white were their wands,
And yellow were the flamboys[1]
  That they held in their hands.

7

He lies betwixt two towers,
  He lies in cold clay,
And the Royal Queen of England
  Goes weeping away.

[1] large candles of beeswax, with several wicks

NOTES TO THE BALLADS

(I) THE FALSE KNIGHT ON THE ROAD

The false knight is a magician, anxious to gain possession of the boy's soul by terrorising him. But the boy refuses to be terrorised and will not even give straight answers to the knight's unnecessary questions. First he says: 'I am going to school,' though it is quite clear that he is standing stock still. Next, when asked what he is carrying, the boy answers impertinently that his books are on his back, and a load of peat—his contribution to the schoolroom fire—is dangling from his arm. The knight can, of course, see for himself that the boy is carrying a heavy load of peat on his back, and a light satchel of books on his arm. Still more impertinently, the boy then claims the knight's own sheep for his mother and himself, allowing the knight only those with blue tails. Sheep, in the Middle Ages, were marked with red 'kyle', or ruddle, in different parts of their bodies as a proof of ownership if they strayed or were stolen; but blue dye was unknown. When the knight loses his temper, the boy turns his curses back against him and escapes.

In a similar Swedish ballad, a witch takes the place of the false knight.

(2) THE TWA SISTERS OF BINNORIE

This ballad is found in hundreds of versions all over northern Europe; most of the Scandinavian ones make the harper play at the wedding of the wicked sister and the knight.

An English broadsheet version for ale-house audiences begins:

> There was a farmer of the West Countrie,
> *Hey down, bow down,*
> There was a farmer of the West Countrie,
> And he had daughters one, two and three,
> *And I'll be true to my love, if my love will be true to me.*

Then the jealous eldest daughter drowns the youngest, but the dramatic story of the harper is omitted. Instead:

> The beadle came and the crowner[1] too
> *Hey down, bow down,*

[1] coroner

With a hue and a cry and a hullaballoo.
And I'll be true to my love, if my love will be true to me.

The eldest daughter she fled overseas,
  Hey down, bow down,
And died an old maid among black savages.
  And I'll be true to my love, if my love will be true to me.

An old maid was always good for a laugh.

(3) LORD RENDAL

This is another very popular ballad, found also in Italy and Germany. According to some English versions, Lord Rendal is poisoned by 'eels and eel broth', which turn out to be vipers. Here his true love gives him toads. Toads are, as it happens, wholesome (if not very tasty) to eat, unless they have been frightened and ill-treated when, in self-defence, they exude a highly venomous sweat. King John is said to have been murdered by toad-sweat mixed in a tankard of ale; it was a favourite witch poison. Lord Rendal's true love seems to have been a witch; other ballads in the same spirit, such as *Clerk Colvill* (4) and *Barbara Allan* (28), tell how a country girl revenges herself on a wealthy young man for marrying, or planning to marry, a woman of his own class.

(4) CLERK COLVILL

Most versions of this ballad represent the Maid of Slane as a mermaid; and there are many popular legends of men who unluckily fall in love with a mermaid, or a freshwater nixie, and get pulled under the water by her. But in the original story, to judge from Scandinavian ballads, the girl is simply a witch. Mermaids do not, of course, either wear or wash bodices, and the green sleeve of the Maid of Slane showed what she was clearly enough. Clerk Colvill's angry reply to his wife, who warned him to beware the wells of Slane, suggests that he had been the young witch's lover before making a respectable marriage. When he tried to resume his former relations with her behind his wife's back, she took revenge by putting a death spell on him. Later ballad singers mistook the witch for a mermaid because she turned into a fish. But all witches with 'a grip of the craft' used to perform that magical change at least once a year (see *Introduction*, p. x); and a mermaid is a salt-water being, whereas the Maid of Slane swam in the River Clyde.

Clerk Colvill must originally have been a member of the cult himself; otherwise her invitation to chase her is inexplicable. Had he agreed, and

146

thus repudiated his Christian marriage, she then would have cancelled the spell. But when he angrily reached for his sword, she let him die.

(5) KEMP OWYNE

'Kemp' means 'warrior' in old German and Scandinavian; and a witch who turns her step-daughter into a monster is the subject of an Icelandic saga. 'Owyne' seems to be the ancient Welsh hero Owain ap Urien.

(6) THOMAS THE RIMER

Thomas of Erceldoune, or Thomas the Rimer, lived between the years 1210 and 1297, and enjoyed country-wide fame as a prophet in England, as well as in Scotland, until nearly a hundred years ago. His powers of prophecy were said to have been given him by the Queen of Elphame—'Elf-home'—the high-priestess of the Scottish witch cult, whose 'gude-man', or lover, Thomas became for seven years. Taking a sudden fancy to Thomas, whom she met when out hunting, she introduced him to her secret Court, and announced that he had already taken the necessary oath to her under the elder-tree, this being a tree which symbolised death in the Old Religion. (Later, the superstitious fear that country people felt for the elder was explained by saying that Judas had hanged himself from it.) Green was the witches' uniform—hence Robin Hood's Lincoln green, and the green sleeve of the Maid of Slane. The Queen of Elphame wore it, and made Thomas wear it too. Nine bells hung from her horse's mane because nine was the number sacred to the all-wise Moon-goddess Hecate, with whom Shakespeare identifies the Queen in *Macbeth*. The Welsh bards called her Rhiannon ('Great Queen') and claimed that her cream-coloured mare ran swifter than the flight of a sea-mew. Converts to the Old Religion had to abjure Christianity, be tattooed with a secret mark, and accept new baptismal names or nicknames. Thus, one William Barton of Kirkliston, the 'gude-man' of a later Queen, became 'John the Baptist'; and Thomas became 'True Thomas'. When Thomas first met the lady by Huntlie Bank and addressed her as the Queen of Heaven, she cautiously disclaimed the title—which had been used by the Caananite goddess Astarte (see *Jeremiah* xliv. 17) centuries before it was conferred on the Virgin Mary —because he did not yet belong to her cult. He had, however, volunteered to go at her side to Heaven or Hell; so she explained to him that these were Christian concepts, which need not worry him if he lived with her—the Old Religion had no concern with either the path of righteousness or the path of wickedness.

Thomas seems then to have undergone an initiation ceremony, such as the Greeks received at Eleusis—fasting, in the pitch dark, and beset by all sorts of terrors to test his loyalty. The apple, in the Old Religion, was given by the Queen to her lover just before his death: a passport to Paradise. Both King Arthur and Ogier the Dane went there, guided by the Goddess Morgan the Fay. Its name was Avalon—'apple land'.

As a tithe to Hell, namely to Hecate, the witches sacrificed a sturdy man or boy once every seven years; and the Queen warns Thomas that they will make him their next victim if he does not behave discreetly. She mentions the 'fernie brae' on the road to Elphame because, in popular belief, fern-seed made people magically invisible—as Thomas is said to have remained while in her service. What happened at Elphame could not be told in the ballad, for security reasons.

(7) SIR PATRICK SPENS

This ballad is probably founded on historical events which took place while Alexander III reigned over Scotland (1241–85). When his daughter Margaret married Eric, King of Norway, she was escorted across the North Sea to her husband by knights and nobles in August, 1281. Many of them drowned on the homeward voyage. The daughter of this marriage, to whom the crown of Scotland had fallen in 1286, popularly known as the 'Maid of Norway', was betrothed four years later to the eldest son of the English King Edward I, but died on the way to England, perhaps in a storm off the Scottish coast. *Sir Patrick Spens* seems to be a confused combination of these two stories. His name is not known otherwise than in the ballad, unless, as T. F. Henderson has suggested, he is the 'Patrick Vans' who was sent by James VI in 1589 to bring back his bride, a Danish princess. One version makes a mermaid appear, with comb and glass, to warn the sailors of their approaching end.

(8) THE TWA CORBIES

In some versions of this ballad the lady remains faithful; as she also does in *The Heron* (20).

(9) HUGH OF LINCOLN

In the year 1225, according to the mediaeval *Annals of Waverley* and the *Annals of Burton*, a Lincoln boy named Hugh was tortured and crucified by the Jews, as a Passover sacrifice. They threw the corpse into a running stream, but the water washed it up again on dry land; they tried burial, but the earth cast it up to the surface; so they dropped it, heavily weighted, into a deep well. When the boy's mother visited the well, the interior glowed with light and exhaled a sweet perfume. She summoned help, grappling hooks were let down, and the body was found. Then a blind woman who touched the bier was miraculously restored to sight, and other miracles followed. A hue and cry being raised, eighteen Jews confessed to the crime and were hanged. Hugh became a saint.

Of several similar murders ascribed to the Jews in England from the twelfth century onwards, the earliest recorded is that of St. William of Norwich. Though all these stories are obviously fabrications—human sacrifice being even more repugnant to the Jews than to the Christians—the question arises: how did they gain credence? The answer may well be that witches were extremely active in the Eastern counties, and that a substitute victim for the Queen's lover, their tithe to Hell (*see note to 6 above*), was needed every seven years. Corpses are never easy to dispose of, and since the victims had been bled to death, in the way that the Mosaic Law prescribed for sheep, goats and oxen, the Jews were the obvious people to frame as murderers. Unable to expect mercy from a Christian court, these signed confessions of guilt, in order to avoid being burned instead of buried; cremation is forbidden by the Law.

The gift of an apple to Sir Hugh by the Jew's daughter, and the nine doors, reads suspiciously as though, in the original version, the boy was sacrificed by the Queen of Elphame and sent to the Apple Paradise (*see note to 6 above*).

(10) THE CHERRY TREE CAROL

This ballad elaborates a story told in *Pseudo-Matthew*, a Gospel that once formed part of the Church Canon. St. Joseph became very unpopular in consequence; there being a widely held superstition that when an expectant mother feels a craving—technically called a *pica*—for any particular food, she must be indulged, or else the child will come to harm.

(11) THE DEMON LOVER

A late and prosaic English broadsheet version preserves what appears to be the original story: the Demon lover was the ghost of a sailor to whom the girl had been betrothed. When he drowned at sea, she married another man; but after three years the ghost, disguised in flesh and blood, came to claim her as his wife and took her aboard a phantom ship which sank as soon as it gained the open sea. He promised to show her 'where the lilies grow at the bottom of the sea'—not on 'the banks of Italy'. The old pre-Christian Hell was cold, and lay to the far North.

(12) ROBIN AND GANDELYN

Although this seems to be a ballad about Robin Hood the Archer, its real subject is the New Year's hunting of the wren in vengeance of the robin murdered at midsummer. The chorus shows that Robin is the spirit of leafy Spring whom Wrennock, the spirit of leafless Winter, has bound with a spell. Robin and Wrennock, indeed, appear to be mediaeval names for the old British gods Belin and Bran, who divided the year between them; in Devonshire, the wren is still known as 'the cuddy vran', or 'Bran's sparrow'. Gandelyn, the bold spirit of the New Year, releases the enchanted spirit of his father Robin by killing the wren. According to a Welsh minstrel legend printed in the *Mabinogion*, young Gandelyn, there called simply 'Dylan', had so sure an aim that he shot the wren through the leg 'between the sinew and the bone'. Wrennock's twenty-four arrows probably stand for the hours of New Year's Day, when the wren-hunt took place. 'Our Lady' is the Queen of Elphame again.

(13) THE CLEVELAND LYKE WAKE DIRGE

This dirge continued to be sung over corpses at Cleveland in Yorkshire until the end of the eighteenth century. Whinny-muir ('Gorsemoor') lies near by. A platter of salt was placed on the corpse's breast, to keep away the Devil; a few grains of salt are put into the mouths of Spanish infants before baptism, for the same reason.

(14) THE GOLDEN VANITIE

There are many contradictory versions of this ballad. The enemy ship is sometimes French, sometimes Spanish, sometimes Turkish; and the boy is sometimes left to drown, and sometimes rescued. If rescued, he sometimes dies, sometimes gets paid the fee—silver and gold, an estate in the North Countrie, or the captain's eldest daughter in marriage—and sometimes is cheated again. The ship-boy probably used the black bull's hide to disguise himself as a dolphin. In one early version, the captain is named Sir Walter Raleigh, and the ship *The Sweet Trinity*; Raleigh was, indeed, popularly charged with having once let a seaman drown, to avoid capture by a Spanish galleon.

(15) YOUNG BEICHAN

Young Beichan is also called 'Young Bekie' or 'Lord Bateman'; and the lady, who has many other names, including 'Shusy Pye', is the daughter either of a Turkish gaoler or of the King of France. The plot of the ballad, a very common one in Germany, Scandinavia, Italy and Spain, has been influenced in England by the story of the Saracen lady who followed Gilbert à Becket (St. Thomas à Becket's father) home from the Holy Land, and went up and down the streets of London calling 'Gilbert!'—the only English word she knew. She found and married him. 'Beichan' and 'Bekie' seem to be corruptions of 'Becket'.

(16) JOHNNY OF COCKLEY'S WELL

The cursing of Johnny's hounds with 'iron banns', meaning 'powerful curses', is forgotten after the first two stanzas; the object of the curse may have been to prevent them from raising the alarm. Nor is it explained why Johnny quarrelled with the seven foresters, apparently his own maternal nephews.

(17) THE UNQUIET GRAVE

The identity of these lovers is not recorded in any version of the ballad. The birch laid on the corpse's breast would grant the ghost admission to the pagan Paradise, the grave being in the greenwood and not in a consecrated cemetery (see note to 19).

(18) GRAEME AND BEWICK

It was an ancient Scottish custom for two young noblemen to swear blood-brotherhood, a pact sealed by each drinking a drop of the other's blood. The elder Bewick drunkenly objects to the pact between his son and Christie Graeme, of whom he has a low opinion. The elder Graeme feels disgraced, and forces Christie to kill his blood-brother.

(19) THE WIFE OF USHER'S WELL

The witch-mother put a curse on the sea, that it would be continuously lashed by gales if her three sons did not come safely home. Witches claimed to control the winds, as Shakespeare mentions in Macbeth. That the sons were also members of the witch cult is proved by the birch hats which they wore on arrival. They came from the Celtic Paradise of Avalon, ruled over by the Death-goddess Morgan the Fay: a pleasant orchard island, with its entrance gate flanked by birch and elder. Birch was the ticket-of-leave granted to the three sons. According to an Irish bardic tradition, the first written message ever delivered consisted of seven strokes cut on a strip of birch bark, to tell a man that his wife had been carried away to this island for seven years.

(20) THE HERON

In most versions of this ballad the 'leal maiden' is explained as the Virgin Mary mourning for her son Jesus. But since the heron is mourning for her mate carried off by a falcon, the 'leal maiden' must obviously be the bride, rather than the mother, of the dead man. It is therefore best to assign this ballad to the Old Religion: the 'leal maiden' recalls the

Goddess Isis weeping over her lover Osiris who has been killed by his rival Set. In the British Isles the feast of Lammas—the first Sunday in August—used to be a day of mourning for the Celtic god Beli, similarly killed by his rival Bran. They appear in the *Morte d'Arthur* as 'Belin' and 'Belan'. When the dead body of William Rufus was taken to Winchester on a cart, the New Forest peasants greeted it everywhere with the sound of wailing; not because they had loved him, but because this was the day when they annually mourned for Beli. The 'leal maiden' has several names in British legend, including 'Cordelia'.

In the original version, the bower was probably overhung not with lilies—the flower of the Virgin Mary—but with 'pervink', or periwinkle, the flower of death, a garland of which, in a French ballad on the same subject, was placed at each corner of the bed. The river, in this French version, was so wide that all the King's horses could drink at it together; and the maiden had chosen the dead knight for her lover from among those who came to the steps of the Royal Palace.

(21) JOHNNY FAA, THE LORD OF LITTLE EGYPT

In 1422 the gipsies emigrated to Germany and France from Hungary, with recommendations from King Sigismund; and by about 1500 had reached England. Five years later, James IV of Scotland sent the Gipsy leader 'Antony Gagina, Count of Little Egypt', to the King of Denmark with similar letters; and in 1540, James V granted various privileges to 'our loved John Faw, Lord and Earl of Little Egypt', and authorised his son and successor, another John Faw, to hang and punish all Egyptians within his realm. 'Little Egypt' was what they called their forgotten homeland—perhaps because one wave of immigrants from India (the true country of their origin) had gone to Little Armenia, and another to Egypt.

At all events, the gipsies became extremely unpopular wherever they went, owing to their thievish habits; and that some of them were wood-carvers and tinkers ('tinker' is the same word as *zingari*, the Hungarian for 'gipsies') did not greatly improve matters. A year after their arrival in Scotland, they were all ordered to leave before thirty days had elapsed; but merely disappeared into the wilder parts of the country for a while. In 1609, under James VI (James I of England), the Scottish Parliament formally expelled them. 'Willie Faa' and three others of that surname were hanged at Edinburgh in 1611 for 'abiding within the kingdom, they being Egyptians'. In 1624, Captain Johnnie Faa and seven others were tried on the same charge and also hanged. He seems to have been the hero of this ballad. There is no positive evidence linking the Countess of Cassilis, who died in 1642, with Captain Johnnie; perhaps the 'castlegate' was misheard as 'Lord Cassilis' gate', and the lady had another name altogether.

'Glamour' is a popular spelling of 'grammar', which meant 'book-learning' before it came to mean 'magic'. The gipsies were then, as now, fortune-tellers, and pretended to cast spells. Johnnie Faa's insistence on being carried across the 'wan water' on the Countess's back is a plausible touch: gipsy men are domineering to their womenfolk, whom they expect to do all the hard and dirty work. When the earl rode up to the wan water, the gipsies at once disappeared into the heather; and, to protect them, the lady swore that she had gone off by herself simply because she liked the vagrant life.

The persecution of the gipsies continued after Captain Johnnie's execution. In 1636, at Haddington, the men of one party were arrested and hanged, and the women drowned—except those with children, who were scourged through the town and branded on the cheeks. In the English Bedlamite ballad *Loving Mad Tom* (24) the singer is careful to disclaim any connexion with the 'gipsies Snap and Pedro'.

(22) KING JOHN AND THE ABBOT

The original story seems to be Arabic, from *The Conquest of Egypt* (A.D. 850): a wicked King sets his viziers certain questions, and threatens to behead them if they cannot find the right answers. A potter disguised as a vizier then tricks the King. One of the questions is: 'How much does the Sun earn each day by his work?' The potter answers: 'A penny: the agreed wage for every labourer who works from sunrise to sunset.' The valuation of King John at twenty-nine pence is borrowed from an Italian tale by Sacchetti, the Tuscan poet and novelist (1335–1400).

In one version of the ballad the shepherd is the Abbot's foster-brother.

(23) GET UP AND BAR THE DOOR

Martinmas, which falls on the 11th of November, was the time when pigs were slaughtered and made into sausages, or 'puddings'. The black puddings contained their blood; the white, such other parts as were not smoked or salted down.

(24) LOVING MAD TOM

This ballad is based on a song used by professional Bedlamite beggars —former inmates of Bethlehem Hospital, a mediaeval London lunatic asylum, whom Edgar describes in *King Lear*:

> Bedlam beggars who with roaring voices
> Strike in their numb and mortified bare arms
> Pins, wooden pricks, nails, sprigs of rosemary,

And with this horrible object from low farms,
Poor pelting villages, sheepcotes and mills,
Sometime with lunatic bans, sometime with prayers
Enforce their charity. 'Poor Turlygood, poor Tom.'

Some verses of the song are still very brutish, but it has obviously been rewritten by an educated person: hence the references to Venus's love affair with Mars, when she was unfaithful to her husband Vulcan, 'the Heavenly Farrier'; and to the Moon-goddess Selene's love affair with Endymion, the shepherd of Mount Latmus—or perhaps with the Shepherd-god Pan—though already married to Phosphorus, the Morning-star. This version of the ballad was probably sung in a Bankside theatre, because '*Sky* bless you all' is substituted for '*God* bless you all'; the Lord Chamberlain having forbidden God's name to be taken in vain on the stage. 'Supping with Humphrey' was the Elizabethan and Jacobean equivalent of 'dining on the Embankment'; the statue of Duke Humphrey in old St. Paul's served as a refuge at night for hungry, homeless beggars. No other play of that period, except *King Lear*, is known into which *Loving Mad Tom* could have been introduced. It may therefore have been sung by Edgar when, at the conclusion of the lines quoted above, he proposes to disguise himself as 'Poor Tom'. 'Cockle pottage', which was supposed to induce amorous inclinations, had given Poor Tom insane longings for his love Maudlen. The hospital in which female lunatics languished was dedicated to Mary Magdalen, or 'Maudlen'. Edgar, it will be recalled, also attributes the loss of his wits to love. He warns King Lear: 'Let not the creaking of shoes, nor the rustling of silks betray thy poor heart to woman!' If the song, which was first copied by one Giles Earle in a manuscript book (1615), does indeed come from *King Lear* (though not necessarily written by Shakespeare), it will have given the scene-shifters time to prepare the stage for: '*Before Gloucester's castle: Kent in the stocks.*'

(25) THE DEAD BROTHER

The speakers are a man and his sister-in-law, who is in child by him; the brother, her husband, has guessed their secret and been killed in the quarrel that followed. The 'little bit of bush' is the unborn child.

In other versions, the murderer is variously named Edward, or Davie, and his mother, not a sister-in-law, questions him. He turns out to have killed his father. When he announces that he is leaving the country, she asks how she shall dispose of his property. He answers that towers and hall can fall down for all he cares—a murderer's property being forfeited to the state—that his wife and children must beg their way through the wide world; and that he leaves his mother the curses of Hell for having instigated the murder.

In the Middle Ages, different breeds of hawk were assigned to different ranks of nobility and gentry when they went out hawking. Since the murderer in this ballad flew a goshawk, not a falcon or any other nobler breed, he must have been a yeoman, or independent farmer.

(26) CHEVY CHASE

The Battle of Otterburn was fought on August 19th, 1388, in the reign of Richard II, not Henry IV.

In one Scottish version of the ballad, Earl Douglas is murdered by a boy with a penknife on the eve of the battle; and Earl Percy, after a long fight with Sir Hugh Montgomery, is taken prisoner by him. In another version, Earl Douglas is the aggressor, and invades the English border as far south as Newcastle, where he unhorses Percy with a spear thrust. They agree to meet again at Otterburn, three days later; the Percy then kills the Douglas with a sword-cut on the brow, but Sir Hugh Montgomery captures the Percy, as in the former version.

The English versions are so circumstantial and exultant—Sir Philip Sidney confessed that the ballad moved his heart more than the sound of a trumpet, though it were sung by a rough-voiced old harper—and the Scottish are so cursory and modest, that it comes as a great surprise, on reading the impartial account compiled by Sir John Froissart in his *Chronicles* from information given him by both English and Scottish eye-witnesses, to find that the Scots have greatly understated their successes. Sir Henry Percy, son of the Earl of Northumberland (who took no part in the battle), had lately been appointed Lord-Lieutenant of the Marches in the place of Lord Neville; this caused a deal of ill-feeling and dissension, of which the Scottish earls decided to take advantage by a surprise attack on Newcastle, with an army of more than 40,000 men. The Earl of Douglas burned and ravaged Durham county and reached Newcastle where, in the course of a skirmish, he managed to capture Sir Henry's personal pennon. When Sir Henry swore to win it back, the Earl of Douglas promised that it would be hung outside his tent that night if Sir Henry cared to retrieve it. Sir Henry did not accept the challenge but, accompanied by his brother Sir Ralph, followed the Scots as they retired, driving captured cattle before them, until they camped at Otterburn.

A battle took place that evening. The English outnumbered the Scots by four to one and, though worn out with marching, drove the Scots back at first in a surprise attack. The Earl of Douglas, while rallying his men, fell mortally wounded by three knights' lances; but this was now a moonlight battle and they failed to recognise their victim. The dying Earl ordered his captains to give out that he was still in the field. Presently the Scots, who included the Earls of March, Dunbar and Moray, counter-attacked with irresistible force, severely wounding and capturing Sir Ralph Percy. Sir Henry then surrendered to Lord (not Sir Hugh) Montgomery, and the Scots pursued the retreating English for five miles. The English lost 1,040 men in dead and prisoners during the battle, and another 840 during the pursuit; more than a thousand men were wounded. The Scots lost about a hundred dead and two hundred prisoners in all; and later gained 200,000 francs in ransom money. Never since Bannockburn had they given the English such a beating. Newcastle was saved only by the Bishop of Durham's courage; he took the field, armed, at the head of all the levies he could raise.

(27) WALY, WALY
The speaker is Barbara Erskine, daughter of the Earl of Mar, and wife of the second Marquis of Douglas. Her marriage (1670) was wrecked by the treachery of the Marquis's chamberlain, who put the shoes of one James Lockhart under her bed to make the Marquis suspect that she had been unfaithful. In another ballad this part of the story is given in greater detail: the Marquis on his return to the castle will not listen to her explanations, but rides away; and the Earl of Mar presently sends 'fifty brisk dragoons' to fetch her back. A formal separation took place in 1681.

(28) BARBARA ALLAN
It is clear enough that Sir John Graeme did not die merely of a broken heart. Like Clerk Colvill (4), he seems to have been a landowner who had an affair with a country girl, but later decided to marry a woman of his own class. When this marriage was announced, the girl avenged herself by bewitching him; the procedure being to model a wax image of the victim, make it more real by adding his own (stolen) hair-trimmings and nail-pairings, and then gradually waste it over a candle, sticking pins into parts that the witch wanted to injure most.

(29) ROBIN HOOD AND THE THREE SQUIRES
The calendar of the Old Religion had thirteen 'common-law' months, of four weeks each; with one day left over.

(30) THE HOLY LAND OF WALSINGHAME
This ballad has been re-written by a skilled Elizabethan poet: some say that he was Sir Walter Raleigh. The Shrine of Our Lady of Walsingham in Norfolk was much frequented by pilgrims; but had the reputation of

being a place where they went as an excuse for love affairs rather than for penitence. A strange feature of this ballad is that the true love remains young and beautiful, while the pilgrim, who has loved her all his life, describes himself as old and infirm. She may be no more than an allegorical character: Beauty. Or she may be the Queen of Elphame again, of whom her devotee Andrew Mann said, when questioned at a witch trial: 'She can be old or young as she pleases.'

(31) SIR ANDREW BARTON

Sir Andrew Barton, owner of *The Lion*, was given 'letters of reprisal' against the Portuguese by King James IV of Scotland; that is to say, permission to take revenge for a ship, commanded by his father, which they had seized. Sir Andrew seems to have abused this privilege by plundering English ships, as well as Portuguese ones, containing valuable cargo, from Africa and India, intended for London merchants. Portugal, under Emmanuel I (1495–1521), was the richest country in Europe, and Sir Andrew may well have captured ships between Oporto and Antwerp (where there was a Portuguese 'staple' or depôt) carrying great quantities of gold and precious stones. In 1511, prompted by King Henry VIII, Sir Thomas and Sir Edward Howard sailed out with two ships against Sir Andrew Barton, killed him after a hard fight, and brought *The Lion* back to London. King James demanded compensation, but King Henry refused this, on the ground that Sir Andrew had been a pirate. Two years later, King James died at Flodden Field.

In one version of the ballad, Sir Andrew boasts savagely, after stanza 39:

> When once I met with the Portingals,
>   I fought them, yea, I did indeed!
> Full thirty of their heads I salted,
>   And sent them home to eat with bread.

The destructive beams carried by Sir Andrew in the topcastle, or fortified platform at the head of his foremast, were pointed baulks of timber, to be hurled down on an enemy ship, held close by grappling irons, with force sufficient to break through her deck and bottom. In 1335, one of King Edward III's ships, *The Trinity*, of 200 tons, had been supplied with ropes for hauling great stones to a similar topcastle.

One should perhaps divide by ten the number of Scots and English reputedly engaged in this fight; and the armament of Sir Andrew's pinnace also seems to be grossly exaggerated. The joke against the Welsh in stanza 54 refers to the needy Welshmen who swarmed over the English border to beg favours from the Tudors, their compatriots. Merchants

157

who made the 'Bordeaux voyage' brought back wine, usually in exchange for wool.

(32) BRUTON TOWN

Whether the plot of this ballad is taken from Boccaccio's story, which Keats later used in his poem 'The Pot of Basil', or whether they have a common earlier origin, is unknown. The bereaved woman subsequently plants her lover's head in a flower-pot, from which a magic plant of basil then sprouts.

(33) THE DEATH OF ROBIN HOOD

The events leading to Robin Hood's death are circumstantially given. Kirkeslie nunnery did indeed enjoy an evil reputation for loose living in the Middle Ages, and it is possible that the Prioress bled Robin a little too vigorously, hoping to please her bishop. But almost every illness was then treated by violent purges, or bleedings, or both. Robin Hood's grave is still shown at Kirkeslie, a very long bowshot from the ruined building.

An interesting point in this ballad is that Will Scathelock ('Will Scarlet') suspects Robin of wishing to make his peace with the Church, confess to the Kirkeslie chaplain, and betray his fellow-outlaws. Will would like the whole band to come along and make sure that Robin returns with them. Vexed by this suspicion, Robin Hood replies that he will go with Little John alone; but even Little John promises obedience only on condition that Robin proves his continued allegiance to the Old Religion by 'shooting a penny'—that is, shooting at the cross on the reverse side of a penny. Robin agrees to this.

In some versions, Robin dies merely from the Prioress's bleeding. Here, he is murdered by Red Roger, a kind of Wrennock (12), and the annual mourning for his death has begun even before the blow is struck. Little John wants to burn the nuns alive, crucifixes and all; Robin forbids this, not because their persons are sacrosanct, but because they are women.

(34) THE GABERLUNZIE MAN

If the author had not been King James IV of Scotland (1473-1513), this ballad might well have remained anonymous and become current in many corrupt versions. Perhaps the gaberlunzie ('vagabond') was a gipsy, since he uses 'the beggars' tongue' and claims to be a woodcarver who sells spindles and spinning whorls, besides deceiving the country-folk. The mother's chief fear is that her daughter will be caught in his company, and 'burned in the cheek' as a gipsy.

(35) ADMIRAL BENBOW

John Benbow, born 1653, went to sea as a ship's boy about the year 1664, and joined the Royal Navy in 1678. He took part in several battles, and in 1701 was appointed by King William III to command the West Indian Fleet as Vice-Admiral of the Blue. On August 19th, 1702, sailing off Santa Marta, a port on the South American coast almost due south of Jamaica, Benbow sighted and chased a French flotilla commanded by Admiral du Grasse; however, despite a superiority of seven ships to four, his captains mutinously refused to fight. Benbow pursued the French singlehanded in the *Breda*, his flagship, until he brought them to action; he won the advantage, but the *Breda* was so shattered in the battle that they got away. He died of wounds at Port Royal, Jamaica, on November 4th; the cowardly captains were court-martialled.

(36) WEDNESBURY COCKING

This ballad, composed in the 1770's, was still current by word of mouth a hundred years later, when it was printed as a broadsheet. Attached to the only surviving copy, is the following extract from *The Wednesbury Times*; it concerns the opening of a new Town Hall, complete with a piano, on June 29th, 1872:

A. Bass, Esq., M.P. for East Staffordshire, was loudly cheered on rising to respond. He begged first to thank them for the kind reception they had accorded to him, and also for the kind manner in which they had accepted the toast. He felt exceedingly gratified at having the opportunity of being present on the occasion of such an agreeable and auspicious event for the first time since a hotly contested election, and when everything that was disagreeable was forgotten, and one could be accepted by all parties as their servant. He begged to apologise the absence of Mr. McLean, who was suffering from illness caused by his residence in India, which alone prevented him from being present. As a Staffordshire man he felt that it would ill-become him to say anything but in praise of the good old town of Wednesbury. In erecting that hall they had set many of them an example as to how affairs ought to be, and were managed under the able presidency of Mr. Williams (cheers). He hoped that the gathering might be only the precursor of a more influential municipal gathering not far distant (loud cheers). The town of Wednesbury had yet to earn its laurels in the art of music (No, no!). He would be the last person to speak disparagingly, but if it had not, he hoped that with Mr Brogden's beautiful present it would soon do so. In the kindred art of poetry he thought Wednesbury might be termed a distinguished place (laughter). He never knew a town with a more famous epic—although he should not like to quote it on that occasion—than the celebrated poem of the 'Wednesbury Cocking' (loud laughter). He would conclude by wishing that the hall so auspiciously opened might long be free for the use of the people, and that the great questions affecting the public good might at all times be calmly and temperately discussed within its walls (applause).

'Spittle' (stanza 1), was Scroggins' nickname; 'Brassy' (stanza 10), was Newton's, meaning that he had plenty of cash. Newton's supporters came from Walsall, a town renowned since the seventeenth century for nail-making. Bilston, West Bromwich, Rowley, Darlaston and [Wolver]hampton (stanza 2) are all within a couple of hours' walking distance from Wednesbury, a market town and parliamentary borough. The church was St. Bartholomew's, a fine old Perpendicular building standing high and traditionally built on the site of Woden's temple, which gave Wednesbury its name.

(37) THE CHILDREN IN THE WOOD
This is a typical seventeenth-century broadsheet, with the inevitable moral ending. 'No love between these two was lost' in stanza 32, has been an ambiguous popular saying since 1622; sometimes meaning (as here) that love never waned, and sometimes (as always nowadays) that there was no love, and consequently none to be lost.

(38) THE BANISHED DUKE OF GRANTHAM
This ballad is printed at the end, as a sharp contrast to the preceding *Children in the Wood*; it was still current as a folk song in Lincolnshire fifty years ago. Despite a broadsheet version printed in 1690 to commemorate the death of the Duke of *Grafton* at the siege of Cork, the original victim seems to have been William de la Pole, the first Duke of Suffolk (1396–1450). He had been banished by Henry VI, but intercepted on his voyage to France and beheaded at sea, possibly by order of Richard, Duke of York (1411–60). The trunk was washed ashore near Dover, and (as Shakespeare records in *II Henry VI*, iv. 4) Queen Margaret wept over it. King Henry provided a splendid funeral. The folk-song version has: 'Three dukes'—not youths—'went a-fishing.'

INDEX OF TITLES AND FIRST LINES